The Parent Survival Guide

The Parent Survival Guide

From Chaos to Harmony in Ten Weeks or Less

Theresa Kellam, Ph.D.

Routledge
Taylor & Francis Group
New York London

Routledge
Taylor & Francis Group
270 Madison Avenue
New York, NY 10016

Routledge
Taylor & Francis Group
2 Park Square
Milton Park, Abingdon
Oxon OX14 4RN

© 2009 by Taylor & Francis Group, LLC
Routledge is an imprint of Taylor & Francis Group, an Informa business

Printed in the United States of America on acid-free paper
10 9 8 7 6 5 4 3 2 1

International Standard Book Number-13: 978-0-415-98934-3 (Softcover)

Library of Congress Cataloging-in-Publication Data

Kellam, Theresa.
  The parent survival guide : from chaos to harmony in ten weeks or less / Theresa Kellam.
    p. cm.
  ISBN 978-0-415-98934-3 (pbk. : alk. paper)
  1. Parenting. 2. Parent and child. I. Title.

HQ755.8.K427 2008
649'.1019--dc22
2008021334

Visit the Taylor & Francis Web site at
http://www.taylorandfrancis.com

and the Routledge Web site at
http://www.routledge.com

To my kind and loving father, Brooks, who taught me to know
my heart and be guided by it, to seek truth and beauty
and how to write something that could actually be
published!
To my devoted and loving mother, Connie, who taught me to
live passionately and told me all my life "you can do anything
you put your mind to," until I finally believed her.
To my son, Dylan, whose way of seeing the world makes my
life more poetic, creatively inspired, and humorous.
To my daughter, Deva, who inspires me every day to be strong,
to have integrity, and to stick up for myself,
the underdog, and what I believe in.
To my husband, Kerry, who is the love of my life and has dedicated most of our lives together to helping me achieve
my dreams. Now it's your turn, honey.
To Dr. Garry Landreth, my teacher, mentor, and friend, who
lives what he teaches and has profoundly impacted
my life, enriching every relationship I have or ever
will have.

Contents

Acknowledgments

The book would not have been possible without the parents' dedication to learn this program, the time they took to practice it, and the love they showed to make it a meaningful part of their children's lives. I also want to thank Michelle, Bryan, Nick, and Robert Keathley for being such good sports and going above and beyond. I could not have imagined even venturing to propose this book without the encouragement of my friends Susan Roos, Sheri Gardner, and Sandy Blackard, and I could not have finished it this year without the help of my assistant, Abby Stubbs, and the support of my friends Misty Shatto and William Harper and my editor, Dana Bliss. I am so thankful for you all.

Foreword

This book is about intentionally building sensitive life-changing relationships with children that release their creative coping abilities. Such relationships are based on parents' commitment to understanding their children. All parents spend some time with their children, but many parents do not understand their children. A parent might react, "Understand my child? Of course I understand my child. After all, I'm his mother (or father)—I know my child." But do they really know how to listen to their child's inner emotional world and fulfill their child's needs for emotional nurturing? Do they know how to respond to their child's emotional needs in ways that release their child's creative problem-solving abilities? These questions are not an indictment of parents because there is no good reason why parents should possess these skills. Their life experiences have not equipped them to naturally respond in ways that are implied in these questions, nor have they been trained to do so.

Most parents in our society live under such tremendous social, economic, and time-commitment demands required to maintain their standard of living that the resulting stress leaves little time or energy to devote to building the needed relationships with their children that help prevent problems as children grow and develop. Parenting is at best a difficult, stressful, and often frustrating process for even the most skillful and dedicated parents. Dr. Kellam has been there and has experienced that as a parent; she freely shares her struggles, her mountaintop experiences, and her wisdom that can only come from having lived through both. She describes her experiences with her son, Dylan, who was experiencing severe behavioral problems and psychological symptoms, and says, "I have experienced the pain and frustration of seeing my child rapidly deteriorate, and I found a way to help him." She then shares very personally how Child–Parent Relationship Therapy (CPRT) training and accompanying special playtimes gave her a way to help her son.

This may be the first parenting book in which the author openly allows the reader to see her as a parent living out the struggles and successes—and what she deeply believes—with her own children. Dr. Kellam opens her heart and shares. The results are unprecedented. "When my son, Dylan, was having serious behavioral problems, it didn't feel as though he and I were on the same side. Every day was a struggle, a battle of wills in which we both felt defeated by the end of the day. I simply didn't know what to do or how to help him." She graphically describes the impact CPRT training had on her and her son, and provides insight for parents into their own children. The result is both encouraging and instructive. Parents will find themselves thinking, "That makes so much sense. I want to try that." At other points, parents will experience emerging hope and will think, "I can do that."

Most authors share what is in their minds. Dr. Kellam shares from her heart. The result is a set of practical suggestions that touch the emotional lives of parents and children. "I realized that the accepting environment I had created in our special playtime had been missing in our home. By allowing Dylan to experience his feelings fully, I became aware of how much pressure I had put on myself to make sure my child was always happy and secure. In turn, I had been pressuring Dylan to be perfect. I was saddened by this awareness, but I was also grateful for it because it was the key to understanding Dylan's world." This book provides parents the keys to understanding their children's world.

The dynamic dimensions of the child's world as expressed in parent–child play sessions are revealed in these easy-to-read pages that draw the parent onto the next page and the next page to discover the process of communicating with children through their natural medium of expression—play—as they play out what is important to them in their world. Dr. Kellam skillfully teaches parents how to structure special play sessions that change the lives of not only children, but parents as well. Detailed, step-by-step instruction for structuring life-changing parent–child special playtimes is provided in the pages of this book. Nothing is left out! Specific toys are identified, and suggested responses to children's play behaviors and questions are provided.

Although not a stated goal, I experienced this book as being about changing our society by changing the most basic and fundamental relationship in our society: the relationship that exists between parent and child. It teaches parents how to build the kind of parent–child relationship that makes the parenting process easier by equipping parents with basic child-centered play therapy skills that have proven to be necessary and effective dimensions in facilitating the development of a positive relationship between parent and child.

This is a book about hope and encouragement and how parents can make an emotional difference in their children's lives by being compassionate, meeting their children's emotional needs, focusing on their children's strengths, and learning how to respect themselves as unique individuals in the adventure referred to as parenting.

Garry L. Landreth

Regents Professor
University of North Texas

Introduction: This Program Is Different

This is probably not the first parenting book you've picked up, and you may be wondering why it will help any more than the other ones you've read. The answer is in the program on which the book is based. With this program, you will learn a new way of "being with" your child that has the potential to heal both of you. You will change your relationship with your child, not just learn skills and techniques.

It is possible to see results within the first week of practicing this program, and it allows you to enrich your relationship with your child in a way that is free from psychological baggage and dysfunctional family patterns for as long as you decide to practice it. You will learn to make changes gradually by practicing this new way of "being with" your child during play sessions you schedule at home each week. In these playtimes, you will focus on staying attuned to your child's emotional needs and setting limits therapeutically.

Based on a Well-Researched Model

This program is also unique because it is based on client-centered play therapy training. Client-centered play therapy is a well-researched model with hundreds of studies supporting its effectiveness in alleviating a wide variety of children's problems. Client-centered play therapy training *for parents* has gone by two different names in the past. Originally, it was called *filial therapy training,* and more recently has been referred to as *Child–Parent Relationship Training.*[1] Both of these titles mean the same thing. This method, whichever name you choose, is supported by more than 30 research studies at the time of this writing, and has been shown to alleviate behavior problems, reduce parenting stress, increase parents' feelings of competence and acceptance of their children, and enhance the parent–child relationship. It has also improved marital relationships. When this program was used with teachers, it even showed gains in children's reading ability. It is specifically designed to increase your child's self-control, self-confidence, self-esteem, creativity, and ability to be responsible. At the same time, it will make your job as a parent simpler. You don't have to work at this all day, every day, to make an impact. In fact, you only need to practice this program *30 minutes, once a week,* during "special playtimes" you will learn to have with your child (see chapters 2 and 3).

I've Experienced Results in My Family Practice and With My Own Children

I know, it sounds too good to be true. As I'm writing this, even I find it hard to believe, and I've had a lot of experience with this model. I have studied the research and even conducted my own use of this program. I've practiced it with many families over the years as a child and family psychologist and witnessed the results firsthand.[3] Most importantly, though, I have used this program with my own children and experienced a profound transformation in my family. Throughout this book, I will be sharing my experience as a therapist who works with families. I will also show how continuing the use of this method over an 11-year period influenced my relationship with both my son, Dylan, and my daughter, Deva, and tell you how they have benefited from it.

I want to emphasize that I found this program when I was at my wit's end. I had read several parenting books, sought the advice of professionals and friends, and tried everything I could think of. Dylan was experiencing severe behavioral problems and psychological symptoms, and nothing seemed to help. I am writing this book because I experienced the pain and frustration of seeing my child rapidly deteriorate, and I found a way to help him. The story of my experience with Dylan using filial therapy training was published in 2006 in Garry Landreth and Sue Bratton's book about filial therapy training and is presented throughout this book in gray-shaded boxes.

Everything I have written in this book is a result of my training in play therapy and filial therapy with Dr. Garry Landreth, an enormously respected professor, supervisor, researcher, author, and play therapist who developed the 10-week model of filial therapy training for parents. Typically, parents are trained in groups with other parents. They schedule a play session with one of their children at home and videotape it, so that they can bring it to the training group for input from the therapist and other parents.

There are 10 chapters in this book designed to follow the 10-week filial therapy training model, one chapter for each week of training. The first three chapters are designed to teach you the skills you need to have weekly play sessions with your child. Once you have developed the skills described in these chapters and collected the toys that are recommended in chapter 2, you can schedule a special playtime with your child. For now, choose just one of your children to have special playtime with and make arrangements for the others to be taken care of. Choose the child who needs you the most to begin with. Later, you can have play sessions with your other children.

It is recommended that you videotape your sessions so that you can review them and rate yourself with the rating scale that is provided in chapter 3. Chapter 4 discusses therapeutic limit-setting. Try not to skip ahead, though, until you've learned and practiced reflective responding and had at least one play session. The rest of the book is designed to deepen your understanding of your child and enrich your relationship.

The methods described in the book can be used with children between the ages of 2 and 12, but modifications can be made for any age or need. Chapter 2 discusses the changes you may want to consider if your child is a teenager, a baby, or has special needs.

It's Okay to Ask for Help

This book may be used on its own or as a companion to Child–Parent Relationship Training or filial therapy training for parents. It's important to remember, though, that all of the research this book is based on was done with filial therapy groups. It's not known yet how effective this method can be without the aid of a therapist who is trained in filial therapy and the support of a group. If you are not progressing as you expected, you might want to consider consulting with a filial therapy training group or registered play therapist in your area.

Make Changes Gradually

Be aware that making too many changes at once may be overwhelming and set you up for failure. While reading this book, it is important to give the information time to soak in and to practice regularly the skills that are presented. Make small changes each week, instead of trying to change everything at once. Using only one of the skills or picking and choosing a skill here and there will not result in the changes you will experience if you practice the entire program.

It's natural to be resistant to change, even when the change is good. Sometimes you will find yourself holding onto old ideas about what works, even though what you have been trying has not been working. You may be naturally rebellious and have the urge to prove this program wrong. You may feel hopeless and want to give up, thinking that nothing can help. You may tell yourself you're too busy or too damaged from your own childhood. When these things happen, remind yourself that despite your doubts, you have decided to take a leap of faith. Make a commitment to yourself to finish this program and follow it through. If you are willing, this program can transform not only your relationship with your child but also every relationship you have.

Taking Care of Interference

There are two common problems that can interfere with progress when you use this or any other program: overscheduling and allowing your children to spend too much time in front of a screen (TV, computer, video games).

Overscheduling

There are many opportunities for your child after school, but none are more important than spending time with friends and family. Generally speaking, if you have your child enrolled in activities that involve them more than 2 days a week after school, they are overscheduled. Most sports include practice and game time, which would mean the limit is reached with only one after-school activity. Some activities such as music lessons can require 30 minutes of practice time every day at home, so adding another activity after school may be too much. Other activities such as art lessons may just require focus during the day they have the lesson. Two activities like this per week would be fine. If you don't limit your child's after-school activities to 2 days a week, it's likely your child will be stressed and won't have enough time to relax at home or play with friends. In fact, many children have so much to do, they don't have enough time to do homework or sleep the number of hours they need to feel rested! Until that problem is resolved, no program will make a difference.

Too Much Screen Time

If your child is in front of a screen (TV, computer, video game) for more than an hour or two a day, it's too much screen time. Too much screen time robs your child of the interaction he needs with the world and with other people. Being in front of a screen is a lot like being drugged. Just look at your child's face when he has spent too much time in front of a screen. He looks as though he is in a zombie trance. If you are glued to a screen, you aren't learning how to cope emotionally or interact socially. That's why some kids who watch more than an hour or two a day become aggressive. Aggressive behavior is a direct result of the inability to cope emotionally. Interacting with the world can also have other benefits; for example, throwing a ball back and forth actually facilitates neural connections in your child's brain that are involved in learning how to read.

You Are Not Replaceable

Many parents have their child overscheduled or in front of a screen too much as a substitute for parenting. Obviously, though, a screen cannot give your child what he or she needs. All the activities in the world won't replace the relationship your child needs to have with you. If you have too much to do, you may be overwhelmed by the thought of needing to spend more time with your child. It may be time to look at your own schedule to see how you can make more time for your child.

Parents Fighting With Each Other

One other situation that will prohibit progress is when parents fight with each other in front of their children. If fighting is a problem in your relationship with your spouse, make an appointment with a marriage counselor immediately. Otherwise, your children will pay the price.

Special Book Features

There are many features in the book intended to provide support for parents. In addition to my story about my son, Dylan, which is presented throughout the book in gray-shaded boxes, there are several other features that have been included. One of my favorite features is Garry Landreth's "Rules of Thumb".[1,3] To find them, look for the little thumb icon 👍. When you find one, you might want to highlight it or even memorize it. I have found them to be a great way to keep myself on track in difficult situations. Dr. Landreth's rules of thumb also inspired the "Survival Tips"[1,3] that appear at the beginning of each chapter. These tips are also intended to provide guidance for enhancing your relationships with your children.

Another feature developed by Dr. Landreth, which is included in this book is the "Homework" section[1,3] at the end of each chapter. Most of these homework assignments are part of the original 10-week filial therapy training model. Practicing the homework each week will help you become skillful at using this model. A section at the end of the chapters entitled "Review of Previous Homework" is also included. This section was inspired by parents' reviews of their homework each week in the training groups.[3] Since I cannot be there with you to talk with you about your homework, I have provided little discussions about it.

For additional help you can visit www.specialplaytime.com. This Web site was made specifically for this book and includes useful materials you can print out, recommended DVDs and books, links to special playtime videos, and contact information for myself or other filial therapists who are available for consultation. The "Notes" section in the back of the book also provides resources on the filial model.

To help you practice the skills I have included exercises for each skill presented. To get the most benefit from the book, it is important to really do the exercises in each chapter. If you would rather not write in the book, you may print the exercises out at www.specialplaytime.com. On the Web site I have also included a copy of the Child Behavior Inventory and the Parent Behavior Inventory, which are explained below.

Tracking Your Success

Take a moment to write about the relationship you have now with your child, using the Child Behavior Inventory form provided below. By doing this, you will have a record of your relationship before you began the program. If you're like me and so many others, it will be hard to believe the difference in your description by the end of the program. I've listed some areas that are difficult for most parents, but you may have no problems in these areas. Our lives as human beings have much in common, but each life is unique, and your own story is bound to have elements that are different from those of other parents and children.

Child Behavior Inventory

What are your child's strengths? (If it's hard for you to start here, fill this in last.)

_____
_____
_____

What is your child's bedtime like?

_____
_____
_____

How is it getting your child up in the morning and ready to go somewhere?

_____
_____
_____

What is homework time like?

_____
_____
_____

What is it like when you ask your child to do chores?

_____
_____
_____

What are the problems you encounter when you take your child out in public?

_____

_____

_____

What disrespectful behaviors have you been tolerating (for example, yelling, ignoring, refusing to cooperate, hitting others, or saying hurtful things to others)?

_____

_____

_____

What is your child doing that is difficult for you to deal with (for example, giving up easily or not trying, throwing temper tantrums, or not taking responsibility for mistakes)?

_____

_____

_____

When do you find yourself overwhelmed by your child?

_____

_____

_____

What behaviors do you wish you could change in your child?

_____

_____

_____

Which of your child's feelings are most difficult for you to deal with?

_____

_____

_____

What is your biggest fear?

_____

_____

_____

How do you wish things could be with your child?

_____

_____

_____

Your Reactions as a Parent

Now take a moment to consider, on the Parent Behavior Inventory form below, how you are handling problems with your child. This is difficult for most parents, because all parents have done things when they were overwhelmed that they regret later when they have a chance to sit down and consider the situation. All parents make mistakes.

You wouldn't be taking the time to read this book and learn about this program if you didn't care. Give yourself a pat on the back for going above and beyond, take a deep breath, and honestly take a look at your strengths and weaknesses as a parent. It's important to remember,

👍 You have to know your weaknesses in order to know your strengths.

Although I've asked you to list your strengths first, it may be easier for you to know what they are after you've listed your weaknesses.

Parent Behavior Inventory

What are your strengths? (If it's hard for you to start here, fill this in last.)

_____

_____

_____

What do you do when your child will not cooperate with you? (Describe best case scenario and worst case scenario.)

Best Case	Worst Case

What do you do when your child misbehaves? (Describe best case scenario and worst case scenario.)

Best Case	Worst Case

What do you do when your child whines? (Describe best-case scenario and worst-case scenario.)

Best Case	Worst Case

What do you do when your child is demanding? (Describe best-case scenario and worst-case scenario.)

Best Case	Worst Case

What do you do when your child is angry? (Describe best-case scenario and worst-case scenario.)

Best Case	Worst Case

What do you do when your child is sad or crying? (Describe best-case scenario and worst-case scenario.)

Best Case	Worst Case

What do you do when you feel your child is manipulating you? (Describe best-case scenario and worst-case scenario.)

Best Case	Worst Case

What do you do when your child is disrespectful? (Describe best-case scenario and worst-case scenario.)

Best Case	Worst Case

What do you do when your child is helpless or his or her feelings are hurt? (Describe best-case scenario and worst-case scenario.)

Best Case	Worst Case

1

MAKING A LOVING CONNECTION

Survival Tip 1
Focus on What Your Child Needs, Instead of Who You Want Your Child to Be

You may be tempted to skip this chapter because you already have a loving connection with your child. This chapter, though, is the foundation of all the other work you will be doing. It explains the framework you will need to be able to express love to your child in any situation, even when you are frustrated and angry and need to set limits. Although you love your child when you need to set a limit, you might be communicating your desire to be "right" or respected rather than how much you love your child. That's because the more difficult relationships are, the more stubborn and inflexible we tend to become. It's just a normal human reaction. We naturally want to protect ourselves from the pain that the difficulties cause. We start to see the person we are having a difficult time with as separate from us, on the opposing side, a "problem" we must overcome. When this happens, we risk losing sight of the person and start to view our relationship with him or her as something we want control over.

When my son, Dylan, was having serious behavioral problems, it didn't feel as though he and I were on the same side. Every day was a struggle, a battle of wills in which we both felt defeated by the end of the day. I simply didn't know what to do or how to help him. When I began filial therapy training, Dylan was 8 years old and his symptoms were the most severe. He had dyslexia but had not been diagnosed yet, in part because he did not feel safe enough to let us know about the trouble he was having.

He was often disciplined for screaming at, hitting, and pushing his parents and his sister. He was angry much of the time at home and often would not cooperate with simple requests. He refused to do chores, yelled at his parents, and had angry outbursts. During one of these outbursts he broke his closet door; in another, he punched a hole in the wall of his room. He argued frequently with his parents and could not seem to get along with his little sister. He did not respect others' boundaries, often intentionally getting in their personal space to annoy them or push or hit them. During the past year, Dylan had also become more and more hyperactive and unsociable to the point of being unable to make lasting friendships at school. He was not often invited over to children's houses to play and complained of not having any friends. He was so hyperactive and so difficult to socialize with that other children did not want to play with him. He was very critical of other children, complaining about them with vague descriptions—for example, saying he didn't want to play with a particular child because he was "stupid" or another because he was "not any fun." He came home from school many days crying, saying he hated school.

Dylan also seemed to be depressed. He was very sensitive about mistakes he made and often would not try something for fear he could not do it. He had a low frustration tolerance and would give up easily when trying to do something, often throwing things in anger and yelling or crying. At bedtime, he would complain that he never got to see his mom and dad, was often afraid to go to sleep, and had occasional nightmares. Dylan also had difficulty taking responsibility for his mistakes, often blaming others for them. He berated himself, complaining that he was "stupid" at times and at other times claiming to have super powers. He also seemed to be obsessed with aliens, often drawing, playing, or talking about them. There was a noticeable decrease in Dylan's frustration tolerance, scholastic abilities, self-esteem, and self-confidence. His drawings were regressed at times and reflected chaos and pain.

At school Dylan was in trouble frequently for disrupting the class. He was described as the "class clown" by his teachers. He did not stay in his seat or follow directions and did not usually complete assignments he was supposed to at school. He had trouble paying attention. He had to be reminded several times to stay on task, often staring off into space or becoming interested in something other than the assignment he was supposed to be working on. He also had great difficulty completing homework assignments and was very sensitive about receiving any constructive criticism or instruction from others. He struggled for hours on assignments that should have taken minutes. At times he seemed unable or unwilling to read because of his angry, defiant behavior. The professionals at his school did not believe he had a learning disability and discouraged testing him for one. I also wondered if something had happened to him that we didn't know about, but when I questioned him, he assured me that no one had abused him in anyway.[1]

Keeping a Loving Connection

When you struggle in your relationship with your child, you can become so overwhelmed that you cut yourself off from the love and compassion you feel for your child in an attempt to get control over the situation. When your child is acting inappropriately, you may think it's your fault because you weren't hard enough or strict enough. You may begin to have more faith in the harsh, punitive measures that society sanctions than you do in more loving, compassionate approaches. You start to believe that the answer to the problem is to change your child into the person you think he or she should be. You do the same thing to yourself, too. You become harder on yourself for not being the parent you think you should be. On top of having to deal with your child's problems, you have to deal with the guilt of feeling it's all your fault. Under the pressure of responsibility that you naturally feel to make your child into a well-rounded, competent, responsible human being, you may find that you get caught up in the cycle of criticizing yourself or your child constantly, trying to make yourself and your child into the people you think you should be. This is how the loving connection we want to nurture and are striving for gets lost.

A Loving Connection: Guidance Instead of Control

To make a loving connection requires us to be vulnerable, to open our heart to another person. How is it possible to make a loving connection any other way? In trying to control someone and make them into the person we wish, we close our hearts to who that person actually is. It is impossible, therefore, to make a loving connection if you are trying to control someone, especially if you are trying to control him or her in a harsh way. Loving behavior and loving actions can guide and protect children, but they don't control them. If you think you aren't trying to control your child, keep reading because sometimes it's really hard for a parent to recognize this problem in his or her approach to a child.

We often make the mistake of thinking the love we feel for someone is the same as making a loving connection. The love you feel for your child is probably the most powerful feeling of love you have ever had. Feeling love, though, and making a loving connection are not the same thing. To make a loving connection requires us to "be with" the people we love in the feelings they are experiencing and try to see the world through their eyes. To love someone is to focus on what that person needs. Unfortunately, when we love someone, we have a tendency to do just the opposite, to try to get them to feel the way we want them to and see the world the way we do. We focus on who we want them to be, instead of what they need. For example, we want our children to be happy, not sad or angry or scared. We don't want to experience with our children the difficult feelings they have, because it's just too painful. If we can't handle connecting with our children emotionally, in a loving way, our children find other ways to connect emotionally with us, and they're not always pleasant ways.

To Survive We Must Have an Emotional Connection

You can interpret your child's behavior as attempts to connect emotionally with you. If children don't feel safe enough or brave enough to make a loving connection, they will make any emotional connection they can. You may not realize it, but having an emotional connection with someone is so important that our survival may depend on it. In the 1940s, René Spitz, a child psychiatrist, shocked the medical community by showing heart-wrenching film footage of babies in institutions grieving the loss of their mothers who had been sent to jail. Spitz explained that although the babies had all of their physical needs met, some died because their emotional needs had not been met. At the time of the filming, it was thought that babies in institutions would cry more if they were held or cuddled. Even though the babies had clean places to live and all of the food and medical attention they needed, they died because they were not able to make an emotional connection with another human being.

Children Will Connect
Any Way They Can

By about 18 months, if children don't feel safe enough or brave enough to be vulnerable, they can push our buttons to hook us emotionally. Around that time, children begin to say "No" and rebel, which often makes parents angry. The most powerful emotional connection we can make, other than love, is anger. Think about it. Have you ever been so angry at someone that you couldn't stop thinking about him or her, couldn't get your work done, couldn't sleep? That's a powerful emotional connection. Anger gives us a way to emotionally connect while still allowing us to keep our guard up and protect ourselves. Children aren't the only ones who use anger to connect emotionally—we all do. Many couples I work with begin therapy because they've either forgotten or probably never learned how to connect any other way.

Another way children connect with their parents is by pushing their rescue button. It is very difficult for most of us to distinguish a loving connection from rescuing. Sometimes children whine when they are trying to connect by pushing your rescue button, and if you have a particularly sensitive need to rescue, you might have a child who whines a lot. When children connect this way it sounds like this: "Mommyyyyyy, I can't find it" or "Daddyyyyyy, I can't do it. It's too hard. I'm too sick." If they cry when they say it, it might work even better. Don't misunderstand. Children may not know why they become helpless when you're around. It's not always a conscious decision. It can become an unconscious habit to interact this way if every time you do, you are reassured by someone always coming to your rescue. Again, children aren't the only ones who interact this way. We all do, at least occasionally.

When children connect emotionally by trying to hurt our feelings, what they're really trying to tell us is: "I have been hurt and I want you to know what it feels like." You may be the person who has hurt them or you may not. The important thing to remember is that the person who tries to hurt is hurting, whether that person is an adult or a child. Whenever someone is pushing your buttons, either you or they are afraid of not being lovable. When children are acting in irritating ways to get our attention, the message is the same: "I am afraid to tell you how much I need to be loved, because I feel powerless to make myself into the person I think you want me to be." As parents, if we can begin to translate our children's difficult-to-handle behaviors in this way, we will learn to understand what our children need from us. If you are feeling resistant to this idea or overwhelmed by it, it's probably because you have learned to think of rescuing children and giving them what they think they want as giving children what they *need*—but it is actually just the opposite.

Making Things Better
May Not Be Loving

I'll give you an example from my own life. When Dylan was 8 and we found out he had dyslexia, we transferred him to a school with a program for dyslexic children at the beginning of the fourth grade. His first day at school, the students found out he couldn't read very well. Just imagine how the kids treated him and what that was like for him.

> My son had had a really rough day and came home to tell me about it. He said, "Mom, I don't have any friends. Nobody likes me." My response was, "Oh sure you do, you have me and Daddy (not at all what he was talking about); you have your sister and your friends in the old neighborhood. They still like you" (also totally unrelated to what he was talking about). I thought I was trying to make my son feel better, but what I was really saying was, "Please don't tell me when you're hurt. I can't handle it. It hurts too badly. Pretend like everything

is okay. Think about how I need you to feel." I would never want to give my son that message, but that was the message I was giving him by trying to make everything all right, by trying to rescue him. I just wanted to fix things.[2]

It's very difficult to understand that loving your child is not the same thing as making your child happy. I could have taken it even further with Dylan, suggesting we go do something fun or buy a toy he wanted (attempting to take away his pain), but that is not what he needed. What Dylan needed was to learn how to cope with having a rough day, with feeling lonely and unpopular. We all feel that way at times. No matter how wonderful our childhood was, that feeling is just part of being human. When I tried to fix it or make it go away, I was robbing Dylan of the opportunity to learn how to cope with that feeling.

Some parents go to the opposite extreme, thinking that if they are sensitive, they will make their children weak. Another parent may have tried to fix the problem with a harsh antidote, by criticizing the child for not doing something right at school or suggesting ways he should try to interact with others in the future. This implies that the cruelty of others is the child's fault, when in reality, there is nothing the child could have done to make the children stop bullying him that day. To go to either extreme—rescuing or fixing—leaves the child alone with his or her feelings, unsure of how to cope with them, which is exactly the opposite of what is needed.

Being With Your Children So They Won't Feel Alone

What Dylan needed was for me to be with him *in* the feeling, so that he didn't have to face it alone. Through communicating empathy and understanding, I can connect with Dylan right where he is and let him know that I can handle or cope with the pain and support him as he finds his way through it. What I needed to say was, "Sounds like you had a rough day, honey." If he knows I understand how he feels and can handle it, he doesn't have to spend his energy worrying about what I want from him. This is so important, because no matter how hard we try, we can't protect our children from painful feelings; in fact, if we try, we are interfering with their ability to learn how to cope with pain. If a child depends on us to do his coping for him, he will never learn how to cope. To understand that we can cope with whatever emotional pain comes to us is to learn to trust and have faith in our lives and ultimately to trust and have faith in a power beyond us.

The Simple Mechanics of a Loving Connection

As stated earlier, to make a loving connection requires us to give up our need to control the person we love, to be vulnerable. Making a loving connection requires us to "be with" that person rather than "do" something for or to him or her. The key to being with your child in the experience he or she is struggling with is to simply empathize and communicate that empathy.

To empathize with your child you must first recognize the emotion your child is experiencing. Sometimes it's hard to understand what someone is feeling because there are so many possibilities to consider. However, categorizing emotions into four basic, easy-to-remember feelings—happy, sad, angry, and scared—will help you recognize what your child is feeling.

Consider the basic feelings being communicated in the following scenarios.

"Mom, guess what! I made an A on my paper!" The feeling is: _____.

"I miss my daddy." The feeling is: _____.

"I hate you!" The feeling is: _____.

"I want to sleep with the light on." The feeling is: _____.

If you guessed, in order, happy, sad, angry, and scared as the feelings being communicated, you are correct. To communicate your understanding of these feelings in the simplest way, all you would need to do is say "You're" and then say the feeling you recognized.

For example, for the first scenario if your child says, "Mom, guess what! I made an A on my paper!" you might be tempted to say, "I'm so proud of you, you're such a good student." However, this response puts the focus on the parent's feelings and needs, rather than on the child's feelings and needs. The problem of praising will be discussed further in chapter 8, but for now practice focusing on the child's feeling and effort rather than your own feelings so that you can teach your child to be guided by his or her conscience, rather than by what you or others think.

You could communicate your understanding of the child's feeling simply by saying "You're happy," "You're so proud of that," or even, "You worked really hard on that and it paid off!" With these simple statements you have shifted the focus from your evaluation of the child to his or her own evaluation of the work and at the same time emotionally supported and connected with the child. You have also communicated empathy with what your child is feeling. The best way to teach children to empathize is to help them experience empathy firsthand. Empathy is the most important quality in a healthy relationship. In fact, it is impossible to have a healthy relationship without it.

In the second scenario, if your child said, "I miss Daddy," you might be tempted to make him feel better. It is a normal reaction to want to rescue your child from uncomfortable feelings and to say something like "He'll be home soon." There's nothing wrong with this statement, but you may miss an opportunity to be with your child in the sadness he is feeling.

Another reaction you might have is to be so uncomfortable with your child's sadness that you try to make him feel guilty by saying, "How could you miss him? You just talked to him this morning?" or worse, "Your daddy is working hard so he can buy all the nice things we have and all the toys you want." It might even make you angry that your child misses his father because you can't do anything about it; you might say something like "I am so tired of your whining." You may feel unappreciated if you are there for your child but he wants someone else instead, and you might say, "Don't you like being with me? Don't you love me, too?" or "You don't think about how I feel when you say that. You don't love me or care about me."

These responses aren't unusual, but they are hurtful, especially when they are intended to make the child feel guilty. All parents sometimes put their own needs to feel better above their children's needs to feel understood. We all try to talk our children into feeling something we would be more comfortable with, thinking all along that we are just trying to help. We all use guilt sometimes to try to manipulate our children, because it hurts too much to hear what they are hurting about.

The most therapeutic response to your child's sadness is the simplest: to simply say, "You're sad" or "You want your daddy." By communicating empathy and understanding when your child feels sad, you let him know that you can handle his feelings, that you don't need him to be happy all of the time for you. There is a wonderful scene in the movie *Little Miss Sunshine*[3] that beautifully illustrates how therapeutic empathy is. Dwayne, the teenage son and brother in the movie, has dedicated his life to becoming a test pilot. He has even gone so far as to take a vow of silence until he achieves his goal, and has not spoken a word for 9 months. However, during a road trip to a beauty pageant that his little sister, Olive, has entered, he finds out that he is color blind and won't be able to pursue his dream. When he finds out, he starts banging on the van they are traveling in, signaling that he wants out. The family pulls over and he runs out screaming and cussing and collapses on the ground. When his mother walks up to him to try to get him to go back to the van so that they can reach their destination on time, he refuses and yells angry, hurtful things at all of them. While the family is trying to figure out what to do, the little sister, Olive, walks down to Dwayne and simply puts her head on his shoulder. With this simple gesture she communicates her empathy and her willingness to be with Dwayne in his misery so that he doesn't have to suffer alone. She also communicates to him that she can think about what he needs and put her needs aside. Dwayne responds by getting up and apologizing to his family and going back into the van.

The Power of Empathy

You may think that an empathic response like that can only have such a dramatic impact in a movie, but I see it happen all the time. To empathize with your loved ones when they are in pain without trying to make them feel the way you want them to feel is to have faith in their own answers, to give them the room to figure out what they need to do to get through the pain, and to allow them not to think about what you need from them or how you need them to be.

In the third scenario, when your child screams "I hate you!" you may be tempted to react by saying, "Well, I love you." This response, though, ignores the child's anger and puts the focus on the parent's feeling. Hate is actually just another word for anger, anger that is out of touch with reality. When we hate someone, it means we are so angry we can't see anything but the anger. Everything else about the person and our relationship with him or her drops away, because we are overwhelmed with anger.

Some parents may feel very threatened by the word *hate* or by their child's anger and may try to make the child stop feeling angry by trying to make the child feel guilty, saying, "You should be ashamed of yourself for saying that to your own mother." Although you may succeed in making your child feel ashamed, the anger and resentment will not be worked through and can do more damage to the relationship and, ultimately, to your child.

If you feel hurt by your child's anger, you may try to hurt your child by saying something like, "Well, I guess if you hate me, then you don't want any of the Christmas presents I bought for you." As stated before, whenever someone tries to hurt someone else, the message is always "I've been hurt and I want you to know what it feels like." You may not have even been the person who hurt the person who is trying to hurt you, but the message is the same. As parents we have to put our hurt aside and focus on our child's feelings. Sometimes that's very difficult to do in such a heated situation, but if you remember the simple steps of reflective responding, you will know exactly what to do. The first thing to say, even if you decide your child needs a limit or consequence, is "You're really angry at me." Limit-setting is very important, but that won't be discussed until chapters 4 and 6. Empathy is actually the first step in therapeutic limit-setting, though, so you're already learning the first step. We are all more likely to cooperate with someone who understands us.

In the fourth scenario, when your child says "I want to sleep with the light on," you might react by giving in. However, if you do, you might be robbing your child of learning how to self-soothe. When a child is alone in her room, without anyone to soothe her or anything to distract her from her feelings, she has to learn how to cope with the feelings she is experiencing. In fact, there is no other way to learn to cope with difficult emotions, other than to experience them and struggle with them. Learning to sleep on one's own could be argued as a child's first opportunity to reach inward, spiritually. It is a time when you are not there to make things better, when she is safe but may not feel safe. It is a spiritual practice that is available to your child every night, if you don't interfere.

Some parents may feel frustrated by their child's fear. It may not seem rational that your child is afraid, and it may make you angry. You may threaten your child with taking things away by saying, "If you don't go to sleep right now young lady, you are not going to be able to watch TV tomorrow." You may be so frustrated that your threats may become more aggressive, yelling at your child or even threatening to spank her. Imagine how much harder this makes it for your child to feel safe and fall asleep. Now, not only must the child deal with the fears she already had, but also the fear of you being angry with her. The child's ability to cope with fear or learn how to soothe herself has not been addressed at all. Only the parent's need to not have to deal with the child's fear has been addressed.

The first step in teaching your child to cope with fear is to empathize with her by simply saying, "I know you're scared, sweetie." A limit needs to be set also (chapters 4 and 6), because you don't want to give in to the child's fears, but you need to say "No" in a therapeutic way, not in a threatening way. Empathy is always going to be the first step.

This is such a simple thing to do you may be tempted to underestimate how valuable or how powerful it can be. One of the most striking examples of how important it is to acknowledge your child's feelings was told to me by a parent who'd had only one week of filial therapy training. She explained that her 7-year-old son had asked a couple of times earlier that week what to do if someone at school asked him to do drugs. She was shocked that her son had even asked the question, because she had already warned him about the dangers of doing drugs. At first, she reacted by lecturing, emphatically explaining the dangers of drugs to him. He listened and walked away, but later asked the same question. She responded the next time by reflecting, saying, "It sounds like you're worried." "Yeah," he replied. "There's a kid at school who's in a gang and has a gun. I'm afraid if I say no, he'll shoot me." She intervened immediately by calling the school and the police. She was relieved that her son had told her what was going on, but haunted that he might never have told her had she not remembered to empathize with her child and let him know that she could handle what he was feeling. Her son was not asking her to tell him what was right or wrong. He knew it was wrong to do drugs and didn't want to do them. When she responded to him by assuming he didn't know, her son got the message that she wouldn't understand or couldn't handle the situation. He may have even believed that his mother was telling him that it was more important to say "No" than to stay alive.

When you empathize, you suspend your need to intervene by first having faith in your child's own wisdom. Empathy alone can make room for children to learn about and express deeper aspects of themselves. Imagine the confidence you can inspire in your children as you express faith in their wisdom and encourage them to express it. It's true that children need limits and guidance from their parents. Without taking the time to understand how a child feels about a situation, however, you cannot guide him or her effectively.

What's Getting in Your Way?

Using a reflective response is simple, but it's not easy. It goes against our nature to use it, especially with our children. When you disagree with your child's perspective, you might be reluctant to use a reflective response. For example, if your daughter wants a Hershey bar for breakfast, you obviously are not going to agree with her that it would make a good breakfast. You don't have to agree with someone to empathize, though. In fact, you may not even like chocolate, but you can still empathize with her by saying, "You would love to have chocolate for breakfast." Surely, you can understand how she feels. Wouldn't it be great if we could eat whatever we wanted without needing to worry about how it affected our bodies? Wouldn't it be wonderful if chocolate candy was a healthy breakfast?

Likewise, if your son thinks you're mean for making him mow the lawn, you don't have to agree with him to empathize. You can say, "Oh, you think I'm mean if I ask you to help with the chores." When you respond to him like that, he still has to mow the lawn, but you've made it clear to him that you understand how he feels about it. Your son may need to learn how to have a good attitude even when he is doing something he doesn't want to do, but that will be part of limit-setting, discussed in chapter 4.

The Pain of Empathizing

When a child is angry, sad, or scared, your first reaction is to try to stop her from feeling that way, rather than to be with her in the feeling. Ironically, it may be most difficult to respond empathically when you are feeling empathic. When you experience empathy, you hurt along with the person you are empathizing with. In fact, that defines empathy: to feel the emotion with the person, so that he or she doesn't have to experience the pain alone. What makes it so difficult to respond empathically, though, is that once we start experiencing the pain, it's natural to want to make it go away. When you try to make the pain go away, you are actually focused on your own needs not to experience pain. It feels as though you are focused on making the other person's pain go away, but in actuality you are most likely focused on your own pain and communicating to the other person that you can't handle what he or she is going through.

Your ability to respond to your child based on your child's emotional needs depends a lot on how well you can cope with your own emotions. If you can't cope with emotional pain, you are likely to respond in a way that protects you as much as possible from having to deal with it. This means that any unresolved emotional pain from your past is going to interfere with your ability to respond therapeutically. This problem will be discussed in depth in chapter 7, but below we will discuss three of the tough emotions and simple rules of thumb you can follow to help get you back on the right track when you're feeling stuck.

Parental Disappointment

All of us imagine an ideal life with a happy family. Our vision of happiness usually includes having children who are beautiful, smart, creative, and hardworking. They love and respect us and do what we ask them to do with just the right amount of healthy rebellion. Our children are just human, though, and have as many flaws and limitations as other people.

One of the ways we become disappointed in our children is by confusing their needs with ours. Some parents believe that their child must be an A student or must be thin or must be competitive or must be popular. Parents' goals for their children that they believe to be in their children's best interest are sometimes based on the parents' wishes rather than the child's needs. To wish that your child will be free of problems, well liked by everyone, and always happy is not just unreasonable, it is also a guarantee that you will put undue pressure on that child and be disappointed in him or her. What children need is to learn how to cope with the inevitable struggles in life, not avoid them.

Many times the pain we suffered or inflicted on others as children is the driving force behind our goals for our children. For example, if you were not popular in school and suffered a great deal, or were popular and looked down on those who weren't, you may act in ways that communicate to your children your strong need for them to be popular. If they aren't, you may feel disappointed. If your children are suffering at school because others are being cruel to them, ask yourself what they need. If your answer involves strategies to make your child more popular, you have fallen victim to confusing your own wishes with your child's needs. Your child needs a safe place—to cry, to be understood, to be loved no matter what. If you feel an urge to fix or rescue your child, give them this safe place first. Stay focused on how much you love your child, not on what he or she needs to change. The rule of thumb to keep you on track is:

 Focus on the doughnut, not on the hole.

Remember also that feelings of disappointment are normal. Share your feelings with a trusted friend so that you don't take them out on your child.

Parental Anger

Anger is perhaps the most difficult emotion to deal with. It always begins with a feeling of powerlessness. Whenever you have felt anger toward your child, you first felt powerless and then tried to get control over your child or over a situation he or she was in. A lot of times, though, parents become angry by trying to control something they have no power to control. For example, you really cannot control your children's behavior. You can try to make them behave, even threaten them if they behave inappropriately, but ultimately it is self-control that enables your child to behave appropriately. You can't control your child's feelings, either. No matter what you do, your child is going to have to deal with sadness, anger, and disappointment. If you've ever been frustrated at your child's inability to fall asleep at bedtime, then you know you can't make your child go to sleep, and if your child won't eat her vegetables, you can't make her.

Are You a Thermostat or a Thermometer?

It's obviously futile to try to control things you can't control, but all parents occasionally find themselves in that situation. It's important to understand what you have control over and what you don't. There is a rule of thumb that is helpful to remember when you start feeling angry and need to understand what you have control over. The rule is:

👍   Be a thermostat, not a thermometer.[4]

Which would you rather be, a thermostat or a thermometer? A thermometer merely reads and reacts to the temperature, while a thermostat controls the environment. Although you rarely have control over your child's behavior, you always have control over your own and the environment you create for your child. Admittedly, it's hard to remember that we always have a choice about how to behave, especially when we feel angry, but modeling for your child how to deal with anger makes more of an impression than any other method you use.

Parental Guilt

Your fantasies of having children didn't include the problems you are dealing with now or the way you have reacted to them. If you've read this far, you're most likely dealing with guilt about some of the mistakes you've made. I hope that you are beginning to realize that the behaviors in your child that are driving you crazy are there for a reason and that before any progress can be made, you first have to understand your child on a deeper level. You might be beating yourself up for handling things the way you have so far. The fact is, though, it is not possible to always do the right thing or to never hurt your child's feelings, and dealing with that is probably the most difficult part of parenting for most people.

When I began filial therapy training, I was dealing with a lot of guilt that I tried to pretend wasn't there. I didn't realize at the time how my guilt affected my unwillingness to be empathic to others.

I came to the first session somewhat guarded, minimizing the problems that Dylan and I were having to myself and to the group. I remember feeling somewhat judgmental of one mom as she began to describe her frustration with her daughter. These feelings were, of course, a defense mechanism against my own feelings of inadequacy, frustration, and helplessness about parenting and the shame and pain I carried for mistakes I had made as a parent.

I had no idea at the time how guilty I felt about the problems my son was having. My judgmental attitude quickly suited me up in arrogance and would have served to separate me from the group but, fortunately, Dr. Landreth swiftly brought my dilemma to my attention. One mother mentioned that she had yelled at her child and Dr. Landreth asked, "Anyone else here ever yell at your child?" His question felt like a blow at first. I was flooded with uncomfortable thoughts and feelings. I was not the perfect parent I was pretending to myself to be. I also was intensely aware of the fear I was feeling about being judged in the same way I had been judging others. I was afraid of being thought of as someone who needed help or needed to change.

The group was silent. We looked at our notepads and squirmed in our seats. My shield of arrogance had lost its power. I put my pen down and crossed my arms in front of me, trying to protect myself from exposure. Then Dr. Landreth asked me directly, "Theresa, what about you?" "I've gotten a lot better," I explained, still feeling defensive, "but yes, I've yelled at my kids." "Sure, we all have. Parents yell at their kids. Parents aren't perfect," Dr. Landreth explained. He continued to normalize all of the thoughts, behaviors, and feelings we thought had set us apart from the "good parents" we wanted to be, and conveyed acceptance for mistakes we had believed to be unforgivable. My arrogance was not stripped away to expose my incompetence but transformed into confidence and an openness to myself and others. Now, instead of pretending to be perfect or better than the others in the group, I belonged. I was part of a group of parents who cared about their children and each other.[1]

Give Yourself a Break

What I learned that first day in the group was to have compassion for myself as a parent. Parenting is hard for everyone. *Yes, everyone.* In today's world there seems to be added pressure. If you're a working mother, you might feel guilty that you're not at home, and if you're a stay-at-home mom, you might feel guilty that you aren't working. Dads feel guilty for spending too much time at work and not enough with the family or they feel guilty about not making enough money because they're not spending enough time at work. Sometimes it just seems impossible to get it right.

One of the problems with guilt is that it typically makes a very bad guide for how to parent your children. For example, when my daughter was younger, I used to feel guilty about not being with her enough. When it was her bedtime and she wanted me to stay with her or stay up a little while with me, I sometimes gave in because of my guilt. The problem was that I felt guilty then because she wasn't getting to bed on time. That is usually the case with guilt. When you do what you think you need to do based on trying to make your guilt go away, it leads you down the wrong path and it doesn't get rid of the guilt.

My guide should have been my daughter's needs at that particular moment, which was to get to bed on time and learn how to cope with not getting what she wanted. If my daughter also needed more time with me, I could arrange to be with her when it didn't interfere with her other needs. The fact is, though, that none of us can meet every need another person has. While my child's needs are my guide, I have to recognize I am only human and am not able to meet all her needs, all the time.

There are other mistakes I've made as a parent that I will always feel guilty about. Just like any other parent, I have yelled at my children or said hurtful things to them. I've sometimes been guided by my need not to feel emotional pain, rather than by their emotional needs. I've put unnecessary pressure on them at times, based on my own insecurities, rather than on what they needed. I've tried to control them, instead of guide them. I've made all the mistakes you have.

It's What You Do After What You Did

There is a rule of thumb that has helped me cope with the mistakes I've made, not just as a parent but also as a human being. The rule of thumb is:

👍   What's most important may not be what you do, but what you do after what you did.[4]

In other words, sometimes it's not the mistakes we make as parents that matter as much as how we deal with those mistakes. We all make mistakes and our children can learn a lot from how we deal with the mistakes we make. You are dealing with your mistakes now by learning a more loving way to parent your child.

This rule of thumb has become somewhat of a family motto and has helped our children take responsibility for the mistakes they have made. It has also helped us know how to support our children when they make a mistake.

Practice a Reflective Response

When you practice a reflective response, you practice letting go of your need to rescue, fix, control, or be right. You are focused on making a loving connection. The following scenarios provide you with an opportunity to see what needs might get in the way of making a loving connection or "being with" the people you care about in the feeling they are experiencing, rather than doing something to make them stop feeling the way they do. See how you would respond to the following statements from your child.

1. "I can't do this stupid homework! I hate school!"
2. "Look! Barney is on TV!"
3. "You don't understand. Nobody likes me, because I'm so ugly."
4. "You don't care about me. You love Susie more than me."
5. "Is Mommy going to die, someday?"
6. "My teacher said I was the best artist in the class! I'm even better than Johnny."
7. "You make me do everything! Billy's mom doesn't make him clean up his room or do the dishes. You're mean!"
8. "What if I go to the party and nobody likes me?"

How did you respond to these statements? Some acceptable responses are described below.

Answers Using Reflective Responding

1. *I can't do this stupid homework! I hate school!*

"You're really frustrated." Your buttons might be pushed in this example, because you're worried about your child's self-esteem or your child being responsible and getting his or her homework done. Regardless of the problem, the first step is always going to be empathy.

2. *Look! Barney is on TV!*

"You love Barney!" You can be excited for your child when he or she loves something you don't particularly care for. Remember that being empathic doesn't mean you have to agree with the person you are empathizing with. You may hate Barney but still understand that your child loves him.

3. *You don't understand. Nobody likes me because I'm so ugly.*

"It just feels hopeless right now." You may want to convince your child how beautiful she is, but stop yourself. The message she will get is that you just don't understand and can't handle her feeling that way. The truth is, the most beautiful women in the world feel ugly sometimes. It's something we all have to learn to cope with.

4. *You don't care about me. You love Susie more than me.*

"You're afraid that if I love Susie, it means I don't love you." If your child is feeling jealous, this would be an appropriate response, but if she's trying to make you feel guilty, so that maybe you won't make her do her chores, then your response would be, "Hmmm, you think that when I ask you to clean your room, it means I don't love you as much."

5. *Is Mommy going to die, someday?*

"Sounds like you're worried." Find out what your child is worried about before you answer his or her question. If you make room for your child's fear by empathizing, he can tell you more about it. Otherwise, you may assume incorrectly what the child is worried about.

6. *My teacher said I was the best artist in the class! I'm even better than Johnny.*

"You must feel so proud." It may make you nervous if you think your child is bragging. The only reason people brag, though, is because they want to matter, and they're afraid they don't. If you're the only one your child is bragging to, there is no need to set a limit. If he or she is bragging in front of someone else, you can set a limit. For now, just empathize. Therapeutic limit-setting will be discussed in chapter 4.

7. *You make me do everything! Billy's mom doesn't make him clean up his room or do the dishes. You're mean!*

"You're mad at me because you think I'm treating you unfairly." You may be tempted to get your child to see things the way you do, that he's lucky to have a parent who teaches him to contribute to the family and be responsible. To empathize, though, you have to give up trying to get your child to see things the way you do. You already know that won't work. Again, empathizing doesn't mean you agree with him and it doesn't mean he doesn't have to do his chores.

8. *What if I go to the party and nobody likes me?*

"Parties are supposed to be fun, but sometimes they're scary." You may be tempted to talk your child into feeling more confident, but it might give her the message that she can't talk to you about how hard it is to fit in. Just listen, so that when she needs to talk about how hard junior high is, she can turn to you.

Homework[5]

1. Practice reflecting the four basic feelings (happy, sad, angry, and scared) with your child this week.
2. Notice a physical characteristic of your child that you haven't noticed before. For example, a freckle on her shoulder or the way he tilts his head to the side when he listens.

2

THE WONDER OF PLAY

Speaking Your Child's Language

Survival Tip 2

**Trying to Guide Children, Without First
Understanding Them, Is Like Trying
to Give Someone Directions Without
Knowing Where They Are Starting From**

Now that you have learned how to "be with" your children emotionally, it's time to learn how to play with them. As adults we tend to lose the wonder and awe of the world we felt as children. The joy and freedom inherent in children's play may be difficult to experience as adults. In a recent movie a father lamented, "I wish I liked *anything* as much as my kids like bubbles."[1]

To play is to connect with the wonder of life. When we were children the world enthralled and surprised us. We were fascinated by ordinary things like sand, bugs, bits of ribbon, water, rocks, sticks, and boxes—especially boxes. They could be anything we could imagine: a dollhouse, a treasure chest, or a bed for a beloved stuffed animal.

You may have been so amazed by a particular toy as a child that you still remember the first time you saw one. One of my earliest childhood memories is of the first time I saw a pinwheel. I can still see it in my mind's eye, moving as if by magic as I held it out in front of me. I also remember my father's face lighting up as I asked him, "How?" You may have had a special or favorite toy as a child, one you have kept your entire life or one you lost and scoured antique and thrift stores for or found again on eBay. Toys become special to us because they help us connect to a special person or place or time. They can help us understand who we are, who we want to be, and what we are capable of.

The way children play with toys can also help them work through things they feel overwhelmed by. Children may not have the words for what they feel or even understand what they feel, but they can play what they feel. As the world-renowned play therapist Garry Landreth explained, "Toys are a child's words and play is a child's language."[2] Having therapeutic playtime with your children using the model described in this book (called "special" playtime) enables you to enter their world and understand them on a deeper level.

Collecting Toys for Special Playtime

To set up special playtime with your child requires a little preparation. First, you will need to collect a kit of therapeutic toys for your sessions with your child.[3] These toys become your child's "vocabulary" during special playtime. Below is a list of the required toys for children between the ages of 2 and 12. Refer to the section on modified sessions later in this chapter if your child is younger or older than this.

Art Materials:

- 8 crayons in a plastic zip-lock bag (no need to buy new, they can be used)
- Drawing paper (just grab some out of your computer printer paper)
- Blunt scissors (I bet you have a couple of pairs lying around)
- Transparent tape

- Masking tape
- Playdough (can be homemade)

Nurturing Toys:

- Doctor kit
- A box of adhesive bandage strips (only three at a time in the box; store the rest in a plastic bag somewhere else)
- Baby doll
- Baby blanket (one from when your child was a baby would be perfect)
- Baby bottle (a real one that you can fill with water)

Aggressive Toys:

- 2 plastic wild animals (a snake and an open mouth shark are best, but anything wild will do)
- 10 plastic army men (you can use knights or soldiers of any kind)
- Dart gun with suction darts (this is one of the most important toys)
- Rubber knife
- Aggressive puppet (can be made from a sock and a permanent marker)
- Toy handcuffs with key (these can also symbolize control, trust, and power)
- Lone Ranger mask (you can make one out of felt or get the paper ones at a party store; sometimes they have them at the dollar store in a package with the dart gun or handcuffs)
- Inflatable punching bag (you may also use a "punching pillow")
- Shoe box, old telephone book, balloons (for tearing and stomping)
- Rope (soft rope is best, but make sure it's long enough to tie you up! You can also cut the ends off of a long jump rope. This toy can also be used to symbolize connection, trust, and power)

Toys for Imaginative Play

- Dollhouse doll family (mom, dad, brother, sister and baby; these toys can be used to symbolize many themes and feelings)
- Dollhouse furniture (bedroom, kitchen, and bathroom)
- Toy car
- Play money (this toy can be used to symbolize power, control, emotional connection, and trust)
- 2 domestic animals

Problem-Solving and Skill-Building Toys

- Ring toss or some other simple game of skill
- Foam ball
- Deck of playing cards

Homemade Toys

The recommended toys are based on decades of play therapy research, so it is highly recommended that you collect all of them. Secondhand or homemade items are fine. Below are instructions for homemade special playtime items. Your kids can help make the toys.

Homemade Playdough Recipe

2-1/2 cups of flour
1/2 cup salt
2 packages dry unsweetened Kool-Aid
2 cups boiling water
3 tablespoons cream of tartar

Mix all the dry ingredients together in one bowl and all the liquid ingredients in another bowl. Then pour the liquid ingredients over the dry ingredients. Stir the mixture until it forms a ball. It will become less sticky as it cools. After it has cooled, knead it until it is smooth.

Homemade Doctor's Kit

Materials for Stethoscope

Hard plastic headband
6 felt 1.5-inch-diameter circles
4 strips of 18-inch grosgrain ribbon
1.5-inch-diameter juice lid

Wrap the inside and outside of the headband in two of the grosgrain ribbon strips and glue the other two strips on the ends of the headband. Glue two of the felt circles onto the inside of the ends of the headband and two on the outside of the ends of the headband to make the ear pieces. Connect the strips of ribbon hanging from the upside-down headband to the juice lid and glue the remaining circles over the lid.

Add a medicine syringe that can be used as a shot (usually pharmacists will give them to you, if you don't already have one), a popsicle stick with thermometer markings on it, and a box of bandages.

Dollhouse Dolls and Furniture

- Magazine cutouts of a mom, dad, brother, sister, and baby
- Cardboard or foamcore
- Box for a bed, nightstand, and dresser
- Large jar lid for a table top
- Small boxes or jars for table base
- Box for kitchen stove and counters
- Small jar and box for toilet
- Box for bathtub
- Box for bathroom sink

You can cut out pictures of people from magazines and glue them to cardboard to make dollhouse dolls. Make a stand for them out of cardboard. Make dollhouse furniture from recycled boxes, cans, bottles, jar lids, and thimbles as described above, and paint or cover with fabric.

Inexpensive Toys

If you don't like the idea of making the toys, you can buy them inexpensively at dollar stores or garage sales. Take your children with you to buy the toys you don't have. If they complain about the toys ("These toys are stupid. I'm not going to play with these") remember to reflect ("You really don't like these toys. You can't even imagine wanting to play with them."). If they cry and scream about wanting different toys remember to reflect by saying, "I know you really want that toy, but we're not getting that toy today, you can put that one on your Birthday Wish List." Say it firmly but lovingly. If they whimper some more, reflect, saying, "I know you're really disappointed." If you are still too afraid to take your child with you to buy the toys because of the way he or she acts in public, then you've picked up the right book. Go buy the toys by yourself and try again after practicing six special playtime sessions the way they are recommended in this book.

Using Toys Your Child Already Has

As you noticed from the toy list, some of the toys you may already have. You may use toys your child already has but only with your child's permission, because the toys in the special playtime kit can only be used during special playtime. At first, my children were reluctant to include their toys in the special playtime toys because of this, but later they started adding all the acceptable ones they could because they realized they were more likely to play with them during special playtime than any other time. Saving special playtime toys for special playtime enhances the sessions by making them special. It also teaches your child to delay gratification—in other words, to wait for what he wants. Delayed gratification is one of the characteristics most highly correlated with success in school, work, and relationships.

Storing Special Playtime Toys

Since special playtime toys are only for special playtime it's important to store them all together in a place that is not easily accessible to your child. Some parents keep them in a duffel bag or box in the trunk of the car. I kept mine in a cedar chest at the end of my bed. You may also use a cardboard box with a lid, such as a copy paper box, and use tape to create a floor plan on the lid for use as a dollhouse.

Visiting Toys and Toys That Are Off Limits

While it is very important to save the special playtime toys for special playtime, there is some flexibility in letting children bring toys with them to special playtime. If a toy they want to bring fits within the categories listed in the kit, then it is fine for your child to bring a toy to visit. Art materials, craft projects, dress-up items, tea parties, play kitchen, toy telephones or other communication devices, monsters, dragons, and mythological or religious figures are also fine to include. No video games, computer games, books, or board games are allowed in special playtime, because these types of activities distract us from our feelings rather than connect us with them.

Worries About Toys

Occasionally parents express concerns about some of the toys in the special playtime kit. In particular, parents are worried about the dart gun or knife. It is important to remember that the toys in special playtime are the child's vocabulary—they help the child express particular therapeutic themes that are difficult to deal with. To limit aggression and violent themes in therapy doesn't make sense, because this is something children should not try to deal with on their own. It would be the equivalent of a therapist agreeing to see a client who had been traumatized by violence and then telling the client, "I'll help you with this as long as you promise never to talk about anything violent." I obviously can't help someone if I don't allow him to talk about what is bothering him. When children express violence with the toys during their special playtime, it means they trust you with that aspect of themselves. Violent, destructive, or homicidal and suicidal thoughts and feelings are not something you want children dealing with on their own. Of course, you will set therapeutic limits on any behaviors that hurt you and your children or the toys or property. How to set those limits will be discussed in chapter 4.

Some parents worry about their children having a baby bottle or pacifier that they can use during playtime. Again, these toys allow the child to express certain themes. Pretending to be a baby allows your children to express their desire to be taken care of, to go back to a time when they had no worries and could depend on you for their every need. When children are stressed or overwhelmed emotionally, it is common for them to talk or act babyish. They are longing to go back to a time when things were different. If your child acts babyish, you can begin interpreting this behavior as her saying, "I'm stressed." If it's not an appropriate time or place to "play baby," suggest that she wait until special playtime or after dinner during family time to play baby. Use therapeutic limit-setting as discussed in chapter 4 to address this issue in a sensitive and caring way.

Occasionally, parents worry that allowing their son to play with dolls and dollhouses will make him sissy or gay. In my experience, most boys enjoy playing with dolls and dollhouses. Typically, boys will comment on the dolls or dollhouses, explaining that they are "girl toys" and they won't play with them. If your child does this, it's important to reflect his opinion, not yours, by saying, "Oh, you think those are girl toys and you've decided not to play with them." Trying to push your son to play with certain toys to make him more tolerant or not to play with certain toys because you fear it will make him attracted to other males sends the same message: "Be who I need you to be, not who you really are." In working with families that have this concern to the extreme, I have witnessed the damage that is caused. Boys in families who are constantly berated or criticized for being "sissy" become intensely ashamed of any part of themselves they consider loving and nurturing. They learn to despise anything feminine, not just in themselves but in others. In the most tragic of these cases I have come across, the family's fear of their son's perceived homosexuality and the intense shame and fear they used to try to change him resulted in his development of psychopathic tendencies. In my first meeting with him, he spit on me. His hatred for me was only a reflection of a much deeper hate his family had taught him to have for himself. No child can experience unconditional love for himself if he is being taught to be ashamed of some aspect of himself.

What Happens in Special Playtime
Can Stay in Special Playtime

It is important to understand that play that is allowed during special playtime does not have to be allowed outside the session. In fact, there are many things I would allow my children to do during a play session that I would set a limit on outside the session. For example, my children can act as goofy and loud as they like in special playtime, but I would set a limit on that type of behavior outside the play session. The main reason for this is that during special playtime my focus is on trying to understand my child on the deepest possible level. There is much more freedom allowed in special playtime because I want my child to be allowed to unfold and feel profoundly accepted. Outside special playtime I am helping my child to be polite and considerate of others and to behave in socially appropriate ways. It helps children have more self-control if they know there is some place they can fully express themselves without having to worry about being socially appropriate. There are so many examples of this. One client I had kept getting in trouble at school for making noises. Once his mother suggested he save noisemaking for special playtime, he was no longer compelled to make them in the class. Another client who spoke baby talk on the school playground after she was orphaned began using special playtime to "play baby" and stopped needing to be the baby in other places.

Behavior Is an Expression of Feelings and Thoughts

All children's behavior is an expression of their feelings and thoughts. If we limit the expression of these feelings and thoughts without first understanding them, we may be asking our children to deal with more than they are able to deal with on their own. For example, in the case where the orphaned girl spoke only in baby talk on the school playground, it seemed essential to get her to stop because it was interfering with her ability to make friends. No one wanted to be with her because she acted like a baby. Even when the consequences were explained to her—that she was losing friends because she was talking in baby talk—she couldn't seem to stop. The reason was that there was a message in her behavior. Although she wasn't conscious of it, her behavior's message was, "I can't handle losing my mommy and daddy all at once. I want to go back to a time when I had both of them. I don't know how to get through this." Once she was allowed to express this during special playtime, the message of her behavior unfolded and she was able to grieve in the arms of her new parents, knowing that she did not have to face her loss alone.

Entering Your Child's World

To understand the world through your children's eyes requires a new way of playing with them, a way that allows them to lead you to a deeper understanding of who they are. One of the most important elements in therapeutic play is to allow your child to lead. To allow your child to lead the play means that you give up teaching, molding, or shaping your child. You make no sugges- tions and ask no questions. That's right. No questions! You may be wondering "How can I understand my child if I don't ask questions?" Have you ever noticed, though, how most children respond to adults' questions? Usually, children shut down. For example, if you ask "Why did you do that?" your children will shrug their shoulders. If you ask "What did you learn at school today?" or "How do you feel about that?" they may respond the same way.

No q's.

When children do answer an adult's questions, most often it is because they know what the adult wants to hear. For example, when you ask your children "How was school today?" they may answer "Good," even if the kids in the class made fun of them and the teacher was mean, because they know that's what you need to hear. If you ask, "Do you know I love you, even though I yelled at you?" they may answer "Yes" because they know that's what you need to hear.

Recently, a mother was excited to tell me that her child had told her that she knew her mother loved her no matter what. When I asked her how it had come up, she explained that she had asked her child, "Do you think I love you even when you're mean to your sister?" Her daughter responded, "Yes," and the mother asked, "How do you know that?" Her daughter then responded, "Because you love me no matter what." The mother had unknowingly taught her daughter to say what she needed to hear by repeating the above questions and telling the daughter the answers until the daughter finally responded the way she thought her mother wanted her to. By doing so, she had actually taught her daughter to focus on the mother's emotional needs, rather than focusing on her daughter's emotional needs.

We all make this mistake sometimes. I remember one night when I was driving in the car with Dylan and caught a glimpse of what I thought was a sad expression, I asked him, "Honey, are you okay?" Imagine a tone of voice that communicated to him how desperately I needed him to be happy, one that was unconsciously focused more on how I needed him to feel than on understanding. He responded by saying, "Sounds like you're worried about me, Mom." We both laughed, of course, because he was using a reflective response to help me become aware of what I was doing. I then reflected, "My worry about you puts a lot of pressure on you."

Tracking Your Child's Behavior

Another problem with questions is that when you ask a question you imply that you don't understand something. Otherwise, why would you ask? When you notice a sad, angry, or fearful expression or even a happy one, you can use a reflective response to communicate your understanding. The rule of thumb for this situation is:

👍   If you have enough information to ask a question, you have enough information to make a statement.[3]

For example, instead of asking "Is that scary?" say "You look worried." Instead of saying, "Did you have a bad day?" say "Looks like you had a rough day, honey." These examples focus on the feeling, but you can also use reflective responding to reflect the behavior by just saying what you see your child do. This is called tracking. For example, if your child rolls his eyes at you, instead of asking "Why did you do that?" you can just say what he did: "I noticed you rolled your eyes when I told you to clean your room."

Sometimes questions may seem accusatory or critical. For example, when we ask "What are you doing with that box?" or "Why did you put that there?" children may become defensive even when we are truly interested and our intention is to understand. Instead of asking a question, you can make an observation such as "You've got a box" or "You decided to put it there." This message conveys your interest and attentiveness without putting your child on the defensive as questions might do.

Tracking can also be used to narrate your child's play without leading. If you are watching your child fly the toy car over the dollhouse you can interact with his play by saying, "It's flying over the top and back down again." Notice, no labels were used. That's because the car might be a spaceship and the dollhouse may be a castle in the child's imagination. It's important to track without labels as much as possible so as not to lead the child or limit his or her imagination in any way.

Practice Tracking

The purpose of tracking is to see the world through your child's eyes without influencing it. Below are some situations that would make many parents want to take control of the play session. See if you can keep the child in the lead by making an observation using tracking.

1. Your child makes the daddy doll hit the mommy doll. Instead of asking "Why is the daddy hitting the mommy?" make an observation using tracking.

2. Your child is organizing the money in the toy cash register but is mixing the $5 with the $1 bills and the nickels and quarters. She is also putting them in the wrong order—$1, $5, $20, and then $10 bills. Instead of saying, "Why are you putting them in that order?" or suggesting the correct order, make an observation using tracking.

3. Your child is playing cards and you notice he sneaks a card from the bottom of the deck. Instead of accusing him of cheating, telling him "It's not fair," or asking him "Why?" make an observation using tracking.

4. Your child is playing with something and turns around so you can't see what he's doing. Instead of asking him what he's doing, make an observation using tracking.

5. After you tell your child that playtime is over she picks up a toy, starts to play with it, and then puts it down. Make an observation using tracking.

Answers Using Tracking

1. Your child makes the daddy doll hit the mommy doll.

    "The daddy doll is hitting the mommy doll." If you ask your child "Why" you may shut down the play. Making an observation gives your child the space to talk about what is going on but doesn't put pressure on him.

2. Your child is organizing the money in the toy cash register, but is mixing the $5 with the $1 bills and the nickels and quarters. She is also putting them in the wrong order—$1, $5, $20, and then $10 bills.

    "You're getting that just the way you want it." Special playtime is not a time for teaching. Letting go of your need to make sure everything is the way it is supposed to be allows you to understand your child's world.

3. Your child is playing cards and you notice he sneaks a card from the bottom of the deck.

    "I see you got another card. It's really, really important to you to win the game." Outside of special playtime it's important to follow the rules, but during special playtime understanding the message of the child's behavior is more important. If the child says, "No, I didn't get a card!" even though you know you saw him, just use tracking again by saying, "Oh, I wasn't supposed to see it. Okay, I'll pretend I didn't know."

4. Your child is playing with something and turns around so you can't see what he's doing.

"Looks like you're working on something secret." Asking your child to turn around or tell you what he is doing will make you the one in the lead. Giving your child the space he needs will allow him to reveal himself at his own pace.

5. After you tell your child that playtime is over, she picks up a toy, starts to play with it, and then puts it down.

"You were playing with that and then you stopped yourself." Pointing out moments like this to your child helps her understand that she has self-control. In fact, you can highlight that by adding, "That shows you have self-control."

Nonverbal Language

You communicate not only with words but also with the way you say them. It's important to become aware of the tone of voice you use when speaking to your child. Imagine the different ways you could say "This is our special playtime," communicating very different messages just by the tone of your voice. The tone of your voice should convey love and understanding during special playtime. If your heart isn't in the right place, none of the things you are learning will help you or your child. It's important to let go of your need to control and change your children; simply love them for who they are. If you feel it in your heart, your voice will reveal it. Sometimes it helps to remember your child as a baby or as a toddler reaching up for you. You may want to look through pictures to find an image of your child that particularly tugs at your heart.

The tone of your voice should also match the mood of your child's play. For example, if your child is excited, your voice will be animated; if your child is sad or angry, your voice will be concerned and serious.

The way you position your body conveys your interest in your child's play. Remember to lean forward and focus intently on what your child is doing. Even if your child has asked you to busy yourself with a toy or a crayon, pay little attention to what you are doing and focus in on your child's play. Your eyes should always be focused on your child so that if he or she looks up at you, you will make eye contact. The rule of thumb for the rest of your body is that:

👍   Your toes should follow your nose.[3]

In other words, move your whole body so that it is facing the child.

Goals of the Play Session

As mentioned above, your goal for the play session is to let go of who you want your children to be, and love and accept them just as they are. Regardless of what problems your child has had or is having or what you wish you could change, special playtime is not the time to think about that. Even though those problems or changes you are wishing for are the very things that motivated you to learn how to do special playtime, it is important to let go of those ideas once you have special playtime.

Another important goal of special playtime is for the child to communicate her thoughts, needs, and feelings. This requires the child to be in the lead and have the freedom to express herself freely through play. Additionally, the parent's goal is to communicate understanding and acceptance to the child. The child should feel valued and experience feelings of self-respect, self-worth, and confidence.

Keeping these goals in mind will change your child's perception of your relationship with him. He will understand that you are there for him and on his side. You will be building a secure and safe place for him to feel loved and enjoyed.

Choosing a Time

You also need to decide on a regular time to have weekly, 30-minute special playtimes with your child. It's best to set a time when you know your child will not be too hungry, too tired, or rushed. Many parents I work with look at me in amazement at the mere suggestion that there may be such a time. Most families today don't have enough time together and are stressed by the thought of adding one more thing to their schedule, especially single and working parents. My experience has been, though, that special playtime provides a very efficient way to meet your child's emotional needs. When I was working and going to graduate school, it was easier and less draining for me to parent using this model. The problems I had with my children often became the focus of our playtime rather than being dragged out all week.

If your family is suffering from too much to do and too many places to be, this may be a good time to rethink your child's after-school activities. A good rule of thumb for extracurricular activities is no more than 2 days a week. This is especially true for parents who are working or single.

Choosing a Place

Once you figure out what day and time would be a good regular time for you and your children, you need to figure out what place would be best. The room where you have your sessions should be private, a place where you will not be disturbed by other people or pets. A room with a door communicates privacy better than an open room. It's like the difference between having a therapy session in the therapist's office or in the lobby. Even if you knew no one was coming into the lobby while you were talking to the therapist, it wouldn't feel as private. It is better if you do not have your children's play sessions in their rooms because there will be too many other distractions. If you have a spare room that would be an ideal place, but if you don't, you may want to choose your own bedroom.

Videotaping

It's important to videotape your sessions with your child, so that you can see how you are doing. Parents are always amazed at what they see in the videotapes that they missed when they were doing the sessions. You may miss how you led your child or interfered with her play during the session, but if you view the video, you're likely to see it. If your child has questions about why you are videotaping the session, explain that you are learning a new way of playing with her and that you may need to watch the tape to make sure you are doing what you are supposed to do. Don't worry if your child is a camera hog or shy in front of the camera. These qualities just give you opportunities to track and reflect your child's behavior and feelings.

If you need help learning how to do special playtime, the tapes can be viewed by a therapist who is trained in filial therapy to help you get on the right track. You may also go to special-playtime.com for suggestions and help. At the end of chapter 3, I have also provided a skills checklist for you to use when viewing your tapes. Chapter 5 includes examples of parents receiving supervision of their play sessions.

Adapting Special Playtime to Babies

The main concern for adapting special playtime for babies is that the toys are safe. Small toys and toy parts (or toys made of certain materials—for example, lead) are dangerous to any age children if they put toys in their mouth because they could choke on them. Make sure the toys you use are developmentally appropriate and recommended for the mental age of your child.

Reflective responses and tracking are excellent ways to communicate with babies, because they are learning language and attuning to their parents' nonverbal language. Being closely attuned to your baby as you are in special playtime will not only help your baby feel emotionally connected, it can also help you to know your baby better. Every baby at any age deserves to be loved just the way he or she is and that's exactly what you are practicing in special playtime. Even if your baby is too young to understand what you are saying, by practicing this method it will become second nature by the time he or she is old enough to really need it.

Adapting Special Playtime to Teens

Teens and even preteens can be embarrassed by even the idea of toys or "special playtime," so you can call your time together anything you want. For example, you can call it by your teen's name, "Dylan Time" or "Deva Time." You can also call it "Listening Time." Maybe not, though. When I read this to my teenage daughter, Deva, she replied, "Ugh. Why give it a name? Why not just say, 'Let's pick a time when we can hang out together and talk or paint.'" I think she's onto something. She also suggests makeup and nail polish for girls. My son and I played drums together when he was a teen.

As Deva points out, doing artistic things is okay for teens. Your "Hang Out Time" kit should include lots of artistic supplies that appeal to your child, or if building is what your children like to do, include building supplies and have it in the shop or the garage, or some area where mess can be cleaned up easily. Another option I devised for a client included a video theme. The client used the video camera to make movies. The mother was able to incorporate almost all of the toys on the list as props for the movies, including the miniature dolls, cars, army men, and furniture, which could be used for special effects scenes.

Adapting Special Playtime to
Special Needs Children

I have taught many parents of special needs children to do special playtime with wonderful results. The important thing to remember is the child's needs. In particular, make sure the toys are safe for the child and, most importantly, put your expectations aside.

Your main focus, as with any parent, is on understanding your child and becoming emotionally attuned to her. There may be particular toys you need to add that soothe, calm, or comfort your child also, such as a soft fleece blanket, a tent to hide in, a pillow to scream in, something that flashes or sparkles when you turn it or push a button, a harp to strum, or a music box.

Is There Meaning in Children's Play?

Sometimes it's hard to believe that there is meaning in children's play. To observing adults, their play may seem random or nonsensical. As a therapist in training I was struck by a story shared by a teacher about a boy playing in the sandbox during playtime that changed my view of children's play. The boy was referred because he was having nightmares and trouble sleeping. My instructor showed tapes of the boy burying a soldier in a mound of sand. The boy then stuck his finger in the mound and made a little tunnel to the soldier. He would then whisper into the tunnel. It was not possible to hear what he was saying, so the therapist tracked his play by saying something like, "I hear you whispering something, but I can't make out the words." The boy continued to play the same way session after session until his symptoms gradually disappeared. The instructor explained that he had no idea what the play meant and that it wasn't necessary to understand it for the boy to improve, because it is the unconditional acceptance the child experienced in the relationship that allowed him to connect with his own inner wisdom and find the solution to the problem. My instructor found out later, though, that the boy had been distraught because of the death of his grandfather. He finally revealed to his parents that he had been worried that his grandfather was lonely in his grave. Somehow, by playing out his worries in the sandbox, he had been able to resolve his feelings enough to be able to talk to his parents about them.

As I began to understand that there was meaning in children's play, I started to look at my son's artwork in a new way.

When Dylan was 8 years old, I went to a parents' night at his school just before I started filial training, and I saw a picture he had drawn (Figure 2.1) displayed on his classroom wall with pictures the other children had drawn of smiling faces. Dylan's picture stood out. I could see the pain and turmoil Dylan was feeling.

Figure 2.1

For example, the face of the central figure in the drawing is a profile, perhaps indicating Dylan's inability to face his problems. The expression on this figure's face seems to reflect intense fear—teeth clenched, eyes wide, and hair standing straight up—but Dylan described him as tough. This expression could also be interpreted as one of pain, considering the oozing wound drawn in the center of the figure's chest. The two faces in the top corners of the drawing are reminiscent of comedy and tragedy masks, but instead depict sadness and anger. The little figure standing beside the big one is perhaps the little bit that is left of Dylan, seeming to be numb, frightened, and overwhelmed.

Figure 2.2, also drawn just prior to filial therapy training, looks more like a 4-year-old's drawing. It is regressed and chaotic, depicting a house and tree with pained expressions and antennae.

Figure 2.2

This drawing accurately illustrates the stress of the family environment at the time. The absence of a chimney is per-haps symbolic of Dylan's inability to express his feelings in the family because my husband and I became more control-ling and strict in reaction to Dylan's behavior problems. The leaning of the house could possibly indicate a loss of psychic equilibrium. The tree leaning in the direction of Dylan's drawing hand could be an indication of a longing for control over his self-being.[4] While the trunk is not broken or wounded, the zigzag through it may imply some sort of scar or damage to the trunk, indicating a past psychological trauma.[4] I knew Dylan was in a lot of pain, but I didn't know how to help him.[5]

Review of Previous Homework

As stated before, a reflective response is essential for all of the other skills you will learn in this program. Continue to practice it as much as you can every week with your child and with other people in your life. The homework you were given at the end of chapter 1 was to find a physical characteristic of your child you hadn't noticed before. The reason for this was to simply have you pay attention to your child, to remember what it was like to be so interested in every little thing about your child as you were when your child was a baby. Pay attention to your child just because it is an important part of creating harmony in your relationship.

Homework[6]

1. Collect or make the toys for the special playtime toy kit.
2. Choose a regularly scheduled time and location for play sessions.
3. Find your video camera, or buy or borrow one.
4. Find a "heart-tugging" picture of your child.

3

A Window to Your Child's Inner World

You have collected the toys and decided on a time and place for special playtime.[1] You know how to reflect your child's feelings and track his or her behavior. You are almost ready to start having special playtime. In fact, after reading this chapter you will be ready to have your first special playtime session. In this chapter on special playtime we set the stage, conditions, limits, and content of the sessions, and then we provide an evaluation template, a list of "do's and don'ts,"[2] a detailed procedures list, a skills checklist, and a review.

Set the Stage

In preparing for the session, it's important to have the toys unwrapped and set up in an orderly manner.[2] You can store them in large zip-up plastic bags or plastic containers so that you can set them out easily and quickly. Some parents like to set out all the toys on a large vinyl tablecloth so that playdough and crayons won't get on the carpet or floors. You could also use a large quilt to define the boundaries of the play session.

From Order to Chaos

It's important that the room and the toys have order. Don't go overboard, though. I tell parents it's the kind of order Oscar (from *The Odd Couple*) would be proud of, not the orderly perfectionism of Felix. The order of the toys and the room allows your child to move into chaos during the session. If there is chaos in the room, it should be of your child's own choice rather than something he or she walked into. Chaos is often where the therapy or healing happens. Sometimes we have to fall to pieces in order to rearrange our psyche in a more functional way.

The Only Limits

While you won't encourage chaos during the session, you won't discourage it either. The only limits you will need for the session are: the 30-minute time limit, and that your child cannot hurt you or him- or herself, or destroy the toys or any other property. It's also important that your child knows that "people are not for shooting." If he or she aims the dart gun at you, say, "I know you'd like to shoot me, but I'm not for shooting. You can shoot the wall and pretend it's me."

You might be tempted to tell your child the limits before you have special playtime but it's also important to remember the rule of thumb:

☞   Don't set limits until they're needed.[3]

In other words, don't tell your child the limits until he or she has broken one or is about to break one. Telling kids the rules or limits before they begin to play or interact will set a tone of inhibition and give your kids the message that you are "in the lead." During special playtime, you are guiding your child rather than leading. So only set the limits when he gets off track, not before.

It's Important

Your child's special playtime is equal to the importance of a doctor's appointment. You would never miss your child's doctor's appointment because you were just too busy or didn't want to go or because your child had a friend over. You also wouldn't say to your child, "If you don't clean your room, you can't go to the doctor" or "If you do what you're told, you will get to go to the doctor." Special playtime should never be used as a reward or a punishment. It's something your child needs. To emphasize how important this time with your child is, you can go to specialplaytime.com and print out a template to make an appointment card for your child's special playtime.

No Interruptions

It's important that you don't allow interruptions during your child's play session. Let your child decorate a *Do Not Disturb* sign to hang on the door during special playtime and explain that during playtime there are no interruptions because nothing is more important than your time together. A template for one can be printed out at www.specialplaytime.com. Right before playtime, ask your child to turn off the phone or unplug it, explaining again that nothing is more important than your time together. If you forget and the phone rings during your play session, just make a point of telling your child that you don't answer the phone during special playtime because nothing is more important than your time together. Avoid any potential distractions you can by letting your child go to the bathroom before the session and putting pets outside or in another room.

Make arrangements for your other children to be taken care of while you have special playtime with one child. It's important that while you're learning how to have special playtime that you limit yourself to having it with only one child. Choose the child who needs you most right now. If you're married, your spouse can have a special playtime with another child or take your children to the park or play a board game with them. Single parents may have to schedule special playtime when other children are scheduled for activities away from home. Eventually, you can have more than one special playtime a week, including sessions for your other children. My husband and I used to schedule playtimes back to back with each child, so that when I was having special playtime with my son, my husband was having special playtime with my daughter and vice versa. This required us to have two different special playtime kits and areas.

Beginning the Session

When you begin the session, here's what you do:

Have your child hang the *Do Not Disturb* sign on the door as you enter the room.

As you walk into the room, say "This is our special playtime and you can play with the toys in lots of ways you would like to." Your voice should convey that you are looking forward to being with your child but shouldn't be overly enthusiastic or fake.

Remember, *do not state the rules*; set limits only when they are needed.

From this point on, let the child lead the session. Don't make suggestions or give permission, even if your child asks you to.

Although it will be really difficult at times, don't ask leading questions such as, "What looks like fun?" or "Would you like to play with this?" Your child can't find his own way if you are making the path for him. Struggling to find our own answers means relying on our own inner wisdom. If you lead your child to where you think he or she needs to go, you may be missing an opportunity to witness your child's strength, courage, and insight. You may also be robbing your child of the ability to see these things in him- or herself.

Reflect Feelings and Track Behavior

If you're trying really hard not to take over or lead the session, you might be tempted to be too passive or too quiet and your child might start feeling as though he's a subject of a science experiment. To prevent this, you can practice reflecting your child's feelings and tracking your child's behavior. Practicing these skills lets your child lead the session and helps you to be verbally active during the session. A simple way to remember to use these skills is to remember the phrase "Say what you see."[4] When you reflect feelings, you are simply giving words for the feeling you see your child express. When you track their behavior, you are simply giving words for the behavior you see them express. If you limit your language to saying what you see, you are likely to be right on track.

Another consideration of being verbally active during the session is the amount of reflecting and tracking you do. All feelings are significant. It would be really difficult to reflect too many feelings. However, tracking is different: If your child is 5 years old or under, you probably can't do too much tracking, but if your child is older, he's going to be more aware of your use of language. Regardless of the age of your child, remember that tracking is used to highlight your child's actions so that he or she feels understood and knows that you are paying attention and are interested in what your child is doing and expressing. Track behaviors that seem significant. Imagine what it might sound like if you just tracked everything your child was doing, without regard to the significance of the behavior: "Oh, I see you bent your leg to sit down"; "Now your hand is resting on the sofa. Now it's not. Now it is." This would become extremely annoying. If your child complains about you tracking or reflecting, it could be that you are tracking too often.

Returning Responsibility

Children are sometimes reluctant to take the lead because they generally aren't allowed to around adults. They may try to put you in a leading position even when you're trying not to be. If this happens you can use a skill called "returning responsibility."[2] For example, suppose your child looks confused and asks, "What am I supposed to do?" When this happens you can return responsibility to the child by saying "In here, you get to decide." If she asks "May I play with this?" explain "You get to decide." If your child asks "Do you like my picture?" you can say "In here it's what you think that matters." If he asks "What's this?" you can return responsibility to him by saying "It can be anything you want it to be."

It's important to join in your child's play as a follower rather than a leader if your child invites you to play. You can keep your child in the lead by asking for direction. For example, if your child says, "I'll be the policeman and you be the bad guy," instead of taking over the lead, simply say enthusiastically, "Okay, you show me what to do." If she asks you to play school and wants you to be the principal talking to a kid who got into trouble, you say in a whisper, as if off stage, "What do I say?" If she tells you to draw something, draw a simple shape or figure that allows you to keep your focus on your child rather than on your drawing.

Show Me What Happens When You Try

Sometimes children ask for help when they don't need it. As discussed in chapter 1, sometimes it's because they want to make an emotional connection by pushing your "rescue button." They may also feel incompetent, lack self-confidence, or be afraid of making a mistake. Regardless of the reason, when you do something for children that they can do for themselves you reinforce these feelings or unhealthy ways of connecting.

On the other hand, it's important to be able to ask for help. Children who are repeatedly expected to handle situations they aren't ready for on their own may learn to give up too quickly and stop asking for the help they need. How can you help your child when neither of you knows what he or she is capable of? One of the best ways I know of is by saying to your child "Show me what happens when you try."[5] This statement communicates to your child that you are there for him and want to understand what he needs help with, without doing it for him.

For example, if your child is whining, "Moooommmm, I can't find the playdough," and the playdough is right in front of him, say, "Show me what happens when you try to find it." Then track what behaviors you see. For example, "I see you're looking over on that side. Now you're looking under the blanket. You didn't find it there. Oh, you found it. It was almost touching you! You just kept looking until you found it."

Offering Assistance

If your child is clearly in a situation in which he needs help, start with the same steps.[2] For example, if a child hands you the playdough can and says, "Here, I can't open it," and you know that your child really can't open it, say, "Show me what happens when you try." Pay close attention to something your child is doing that is on the right track and then highlight it by saying, "I see you've got your fingers under the lid and you're pulling" and then add, "You keep doing that and I'll pull on this side." Then when the lid comes off, say "You did it!" The outline below shows a simple series of steps.

When the child asks for specific help, help the child help himself or herself:

1. Say, "Show me what happens when you try."
2. Use tracking to point out your child's problem-solving process—thoughts and actions.

3. During your child's attempt, share the work: "While you're doing that, I'll do this…"

4. When the task is accomplished, point out success: "You did it!"

Self-Esteem Building Responses[3]

Saying "You did it!" whenever your child accomplishes a task she set out to do increases her feelings of competence and facilitates self-esteem. Self-esteem is so important that it will be discussed more in depth in chapter 8. Other responses you have learned that you can use in your session that enhance your child's self-esteem include:

You're getting that just the way you want it. You can say this when your child is lining up the army soldiers one at a time or arranging dollhouse furniture or cooking a pretend supper.

You noticed… You can say this on so many occasions. If your child says, "You're talking differently," "You changed clothes," or "These are not my toys."

You decided… or *You get to decide.* You can say this when your child announces what he is going to do or when he asks for permission.

You stopped yourself. Say this when your child is about to do something he isn't supposed to do but stops himself.

In here, it's what you think that matters. Say this when your child wants to know what you or someone else thinks.

You figured that out. Say this when your child figures out how to do something or when he tells you how to do something you already know how to do.

These responses salute the child's power and effort rather than praise or criticize what the child does.

👍   Don't answer questions that haven't been asked.[3]

Answering questions during the play session can be a little tricky at first. Whenever a child asks a question, you need to consider his or her motivation. For example, if a child asks, "Did you really like that antique vase that used to be on the table?" He's obviously not asking you the question that it sounds like he's asking. To simply respond by saying "Yes" or "No" would not get to the heart of the matter. An appropriate reflective response would be, "Sounds like you're worried" because what he is really asking is, "Can you forgive me for breaking the antique vase that I know you love so much?"

It's really difficult not to answer questions during special playtime, because as adults taking care of children we like to have all of the answers. It makes us feel competent and in charge. Generally speaking during playtime your job is to be "dumb" for 30 minutes. When your child asks you how to do something or what to do, you can ponder with him by saying, "Hmmm, I wonder how that works." Or you can return responsibility by saying, "In here, you get to decide" or "In here, it can be any way you want it to be." There are some questions you can answer during the session. Any question that would be the same when you respond using reflective listening would probably be a question you can answer directly. For example, if your child asks, "Is daddy going to be home for supper?" and you respond by reflecting, "You're hoping to see daddy tonight." Your child will probably say, "Yeah, is he coming home for supper?" Or if your child asks, "What time is it?" You may respond by reflecting, "You're wondering how much time we have left in our playtime." Your child will probably respond, "Yeah, what time is it?" This rule of thumb doesn't always apply, though. For example, if your child asks, "Do you like this picture?" and you respond by reflecting, "It's really important to you that I like it." Your child may respond by saying, "Yeah, do you like it?" In this case you would respond by saying, "In here, it's what you think that matters. You get to decide if it's a good picture or not."

When I first learned about this I was skeptical. I was frustrated that I couldn't answer the questions that were asked in play sessions. One little girl changed my mind, though. She was one of my first play therapy clients. She had recently been separated from everyone she loved—her mother and father, grandmother and grandfather, and little brother. Early in our session, she held up a can of play food with the label off and asked, "What's this?" I wanted so badly to answer, "It's a can of play food with the label off," but I was being videotaped for class, so I reluctantly complied with instructions by saying, "In here, it can be anything you want it to be." The little girl's face lit up and she said, "Okay, it's a turkey and we're having Thanksgiving and my mother and father and grandmother and grandfather and little brother are going to be there!" I realized that the little girl wasn't asking what I thought she was asking. What she really wanted to know is if she could use her imagination in our sessions together.

Ending the Play Session

It's important to use a clock or watch to set a limit on the time, rather than using a timer. You want your child to know you are responsible for keeping track of the time and for setting the limit. Rather than saying, "Oh darn it, that timer went off, so we have to stop," you would say, "Our time is up for today." Be sure to give a 5-minute warning, though, beforehand by simply saying, "We have 5 minutes left in our special playtime." Be sure not to make any suggestions about what your child should do with the last 5 minutes. Even if your child starts something new that he can't finish, it's important to let him decide. After all, he may be working on dealing with disappointment or self-control and if you try to keep him from being disappointed, you've taken that opportunity away from him.

Your child may be reluctant to leave the session. If he is, remember to reflect first. Say in a loving voice, not an irritated or harsh voice, "You want to keep playing" or "You had a good time and don't want to stop," then add in the same voice, making sure you are also firm, "but our time is up for today. We will have special playtime the same time next week." If your child persists, continue in the same tone of voice, repeating the same words while you stand up. If your child continues, remain calm and continue to reflect while you pick up the toys.

This may be the most frustrating time and therefore the most difficult of the play session. It's important not to undo all of the good work you've done by yelling or shaming or threatening your child. In fact, it's so important that you may want to make things easier for yourself by setting up a surprise you know your child will want after the session, such as milk and cookies or a DVD.

Evaluating Your Sessions

It's important to videotape your sessions with your child so that you can critique your skills. Once you set up the camera, though, don't mess with it. Even if you and your child move out of the camera range, the audio will still work. There are three tables provided at the end of this chapter. Table 3.1 is a summary of the do's and don'ts for your play session. It is helpful to refer to this summary if you have any questions about what you should or shouldn't do when you're evaluating your videotape. Table 3.2 is a procedure checklist to help you stay on track. Table 3.3 is a skills checklist to help you evaluate your progress.

Are You Ready?

You have read about all the skills you need to start your play sessions, but you still need to practice them. Below are some exercises and excerpts from play sessions that will help you master the skills you need. You may have noticed that you haven't yet learned limit-setting, genuine expression, or identifying play themes. You can start your sessions without knowing these skills. It is very important that you be as genuine as you can be during sessions, but in some ways genuineness is an advanced skill that will come with practice and a deeper understanding of the process. Limit-setting will be discussed in the next chapter. Genuineness will be discussed in chapter 5 and chapter 8, and play themes will be discussed in chapter 9.

Review

1. What do you need to do before the play session?
2. What do you say as you enter the room?
3. Should you let your child know the limits before he or she breaks them?
4. What do you do if someone rings the doorbell during your play session?
5. Is it okay for other children or adults or pets to join your play session with your child?
6. What are your goals for the session?
7. How do you end the session?

Answers to Review

1. *What do you need to do before the play session?*

    While you are setting up the toys in a predictable way, have your child use the bathroom. Make sure you have the clock or a watch out where you can see it and set up the video camera. Put the pets outside or in another room and arrange for your other children to be taken care of. Let your child unplug the phone while you explain that "Nothing is more important than our time together" and allow him or her to put the Do Not Disturb sign on the door just before you walk in for the session.

2. *What do you say as you enter the room?*

"This is our special playtime and you can play with the toys in lots of the ways you want to." Remember, you don't tell your child that he can play with the toys in any way he likes, because there are limits on not breaking or destroying the toys or hurting you or himself.

3. *Should you let your child know the limits before he or she breaks them?*

No. Limits are not needed until the limit is being broken.

4. *What do you do if someone rings the doorbell during your play session?*

Don't answer it. If your child gets up to answer the door, remind him that "Nothing is more important than our time together."

5. *Is it okay for other children or adults or pets to join your play session with your child?*

No, this is a time for just you and your child.

6. *What are your goals for the session?*

Simply to love and understand your child on the deepest possible level by letting your child show you who she is.

7. *How do you end the session?*

Five minutes before the session is over you announce, "We have 5 minutes left in our special playtime." As always, you should not give any directions or make any suggestions about how your child should use the last few minutes.

Play Session Transcripts

A Child Who Wants to Please

Mom: This is our special playtime and you can play with the toys in lots of the ways you would like to.

Child: What do you want to do?

Mom: In here you get to decide what to do.

Child: But I want to know what you want to do.

Mom: Hmm, maybe you're worried about me having fun or maybe it's hard to make a decision.

Child: Wanna play cards?

Mom: Sounds like you decided.

Child: Okay… (Hesitates). Can I play with the dollhouse first?

Mom: You get to decide, sweetie.

Child: (Smiles and starts to arrange the furniture) Can you play with me? (Asks hesitantly)

Mom: Okay, you show me what to do.

Child: You can be the mom.

Mom: Oh, okay, I'm the mom. (Holds the mom doll and looks at the child as if ready to take direction)

A Rebellious Child

Mom: This is our special playtime and you can play with the toys in lots of the ways you would like to.

Child: (Walks in with arms crossed, head down, sits down on the floor, frowning, and won't look up.)

Mom: You look upset.

Child: (No verbal response, just crosses arms tighter and sticks out lower lip.)

Mom: Your arms are crossed really tight and your lip is out really far. You want me to know you don't like this.

Child: (Yelling) I wanna play video games!

Mom: Oh, you're disappointed there aren't any video games in here.

Child: (Yelling) These toys are stupid. These are stupid baby toys. I'm never going to play with them.

Mom: Oh, you don't like these toys and you've decided you aren't going to play with them.

Our First Playtime

I expected that the first special playtime I had would have no real impact because I had already used client-centered techniques at home every day. But my relationship with Dylan was changed forever during the first part of the session. The most poignant moment was when Dylan stated that he was going to play 52 Pick-up with the deck of cards.

Dylan: (Looks at his mother before scattering the cards, as if to ask permission.)

Mother: Oh, you've decided what you want to do with those cards.

Dylan: I can do it?

Mother: You get to decide what to do.

Dylan: (Gleefully scatters the cards then says) I'll pick them up.

Mother: Oh, you've decided to pick up the cards.

Dylan: (He picks up a couple more cards, nodding, saying) Uh huh (then suddenly stops, surprised and elated, saying) Oh, I decide not to pick them up! (and scatters those he had gathered).

I had become very strict at home as a reaction to Dylan's hostile behavior. What he needed, however, was some way to express the turmoil he felt inside. I didn't realize it at the time, but the moment described above seemed to symbolize Dylan's need for permission to express the chaos he had been experiencing internally. It was difficult for me to even acknowledge Dylan's internal chaos at this point because I was still caught up in the belief that if my son experienced inner turmoil, it meant that I had been a bad parent and that I didn't have any business being a therapist.

Despite my need to protect myself from Dylan's true feelings, he was able to express them—and even have them acknowledged on some level—due to the structure of the responses I used during the play sessions. He was greatly freed and relieved by the experience. He was also grateful for it and began to express warm and affectionate feelings toward me for perhaps the first time in a very long time. Dylan began to improve dramatically after the first session. During the second playtime a week later, he tenderly held my wrist and designed a bracelet for me. I was deeply touched by the love I felt from him. I realized that the accepting environment I had created in our special playtime had been missing in our home. By allowing Dylan to experience his feelings fully, I became aware of how much pressure I had put on myself to make sure my child was always happy and secure. In turn, I had been pressuring Dylan to be perfect. I was saddened by this awareness, but I also was grateful for it because it was the key to understanding Dylan's world.[6]

Practice Play Session Scenarios

Respond to the following scenarios using the skills you've learned so far:

Your child walks in and sits down with his arms folded and says, "This is stupid! I'm not going to play with these toys."
Your response: "You don't like this one bit." (Your voice should convey understanding and acceptance of how your child feels.)

Your child rolls the ball to you.
Your response: "You rolled it right to me." (Your voice should convey how much you love and value your child.)

Your child asks, "What am I supposed to do?"
Your response: "You get to decide what to do." (Your voice should convey that you are giving your child a gift.)

Your child stabs the baby doll with a knife.

> *Your response*: "You stabbed the doll." (Your voice should convey thoughtful consideration.)

Your child asks, "How much time do we have left?"

> *Your response*: "We have 12 minutes left." (You can answer questions such as this one.)

Your child looks bored.

> *Your response*: "Looks like you're bored." (Your voice should convey love and acceptance.)

Your child rolls the car up your arm, over your head, and down your other arm.

> *Your response*: "That's going up, up, up. Now it's right on top and now it's going down." (You voice should convey how much you value your child's play and interaction with you.)

Your child asks "What does this say?" pointing to a word on a can of play food.

> *Your response*: "In here, you get to decide what it says." (Your voice should convey to your child that you are giving him a gift.)

Your child begins to rearrange the dollhouse furniture, explaining that somebody put the furniture in the wrong room. She then puts the toilet and bathtub in the kitchen, the bedroom furniture in the living room, and the baby bed in the garage.

> *Your response*: "You're getting that all fixed up, just the way you want it."

Your child asks you to join in a game of ring toss. While you're playing she explains that she gets a point for almost getting the ring on the stick; when you do the same thing, she says you don't get a point.

> *Your response*: "Oh, the rules are different for me." (Your voice should convey love and acceptance.)

Table 3.1   Do's and Don'ts for Play Sessions[2a]

Do	Don't
1. Do set the stage.	1. Don't criticize any behavior.
2. Do let the child lead.	2. Don't praise the child.
3. Do track behavior.	3. Don't ask leading questions.
4. Do reflect the child's feelings.	4. Don't allow interruptions of the session.
5. Do set limits.	5. Don't give information or teach.
6. Do salute the child's power and effort.	6. Don't preach.
7. Do join in the play as a follower.	7. Don't initiate new behavior.
8. Do be verbally active.	8. Don't be passive or quiet.

Check Your Responses to Your Children

Your responses should convey:	Your responses *should not* convey:
1. I am here.	1. I always agree.
2. I hear and see you.	2. I must make you happy.
3. I understand.	3. I will solve your problems.
4. I care.	

Table 3.2   Detailed Procedures for Play Sessions[2]

Exact Procedure

- Let the child use the bathroom prior to the play session.
- Have a clock visible in room.
- Keep the toy placement predictable.
- Switch on the video recorder.
- Hang the "Do Not Disturb" sign.
- Say, "This is our special playtime. In here, you can play with the toys in lots of the ways you want to."
- From this point, let the child lead.
- Allow the child to identify the toys and introduce his or her own labels for them.
- Use nonspecific words (this, that, it, there, etc.) or the child's own labels.
- Play actively with the child if the child requests your participation.
- Verbally track the child's behaviors and use reflective responses.
- Set limits on behaviors that make you feel uncomfortable.
- Give 5-minute advance notice for session end.
- At 30 minutes, stand and announce, "Our playtime is over for today."
- Do not exceed 30-minute time limit by more than 2 to 3 minutes.
- Parent does the cleaning up. If child chooses to, child may help.

If Child Has Difficulty Leaving:

- Open the door, begin to put away toys.
- Reflect feelings and wants of the child and restate limit as many times as needed.
- "I know you would like to stay and play with the toys. Our playtime is over for today. You may play with the toys here next time."
- Reflect observations of self-control.
- "You really wanted to finish that and you stopped yourself!"

Table 3.3 Skills Checklist

SKILLS	TOO MUCH	APPROPRIATE	NEED MORE	MISSING	EXAMPLES/ COMMENTS (*STAR YOUR STRENGTHS)
Lean forward/ open					
Relaxed/ comfortable					
Appear interested					
Tracking behavior					
Reflecting feelings					
Returning responsibility					
Rate of responses					
Match child's tone/intensity					
Genuine expression					
See world through child's eyes					
Limit-setting					

Source: Developed by the Center for Play Therapy at the University of North Texas in Denton, Texas.

1. What themes were identified?

_____

_____

2. What feelings did I have during this session?

_____

_____

Review of Previous Homework

By now you should have all of the toys for your special playtime kit. Remember not to let your child play with the toys during the week. They are only for special playtime.

Continue to reflect your child's feelings and track your child's behavior this week and when you do, think of the heart-tugging picture. Try to keep that heart-tugging picture of your child in your mind as much as possible, especially when he or she is pushing your buttons.

Homework[6]

1. Review the "do's and don'ts" and the procedure for special playtime.
2. Have special playtime with your child and don't forget to record it!
3. Review your session using the evaluation provided. You haven't learned everything on the evaluation yet, so keep reading!

4

PROMOTING YOUR CHILD'S EMOTIONAL MATURITY

> **Survival Tip 4**
>
> **Children Who Get Everything They Want Are Not Getting What They Need**

As parents, we often make the mistake of trying to control things we have no control over. For example, parents often make the mistake of trying to control their children's feelings. The problem is, though, you can't control your child's feelings. In fact, you really can't control your own feelings. You cannot choose your feelings. You can distract yourself from them or tell yourself you don't feel a certain way when you actually do, but the more you try to convince yourself you aren't feeling something you don't want to feel, the more likely the emotion will take charge of your life.

Most people deny this reality. It is disconcerting to realize that we actually have no control over how we feel. In fact, most of us have spent a great deal of energy trying to prove that we, or someone else, should have emotional control. The fact is, you can only have control over how you behave, not how you feel.

If you are still struggling with this idea, think back to a time when you were in love with someone who wasn't good for you. Most of us have experienced the agony of being in love with the wrong person. In that situation, no matter how much you try to convince yourself you are not in love with the person, you are powerless to deny the feeling. Perhaps you have been in the opposite situation too, unable to be in love with someone who would be a perfect mate for you. If we could actually choose who we fall in love with, arranged marriages would be more popular than they are.

If we could simply choose our emotions, life would probably be a lot easier. Divorce would be unheard of, because instead of being angry or disappointed with one's spouse, we could just choose to feel happy and proud. No one would prescribe antidepressants or antianxiety medication because we could just choose not to be sad or anxious. Fear of public speaking would be easily overcome by just simply deciding to be calm in front of an audience.

If you have a fear of public speaking, then you truly understand how impossible it is to choose or control your feelings. No matter how much you try, you cannot choose how to feel or to control the powerful, sometimes overwhelming, physiological reactions you have to your emotions in front of an audience. There are so many examples of the difficulties we struggle with because we are not able to choose or control our emotions that it would be impossible to list them all.

I am not saying that if you feel sad, you have to give in to it. In fact, I am saying just the opposite: that it is possible to experience the sadness and still choose to go to work, have a good attitude, or be kind. You always have a choice of how to behave, regardless of the emotions you experience.

Emotions as a Guide

Emotions are not only impossible to choose or control, they are also very mysterious. We can't really say where they come from. Some psychological theories have tried to explain emotions as simply coming from thoughts. These theories are still practiced today and represent a more modern version of discounting emotional or intuitive reasoning.

Earlier theories tried to explain emotions as merely learned or conditioned responses to stimuli. The problem with these theories is that they are based on logic without emotion. It may sound strange to say that logic without emotion could be problematic because we are used to hearing the opposite, which is also true. However, the history of psychology is fraught with tragic examples of how important it is to integrate intuitive or emotional reasoning with logical reasoning. In particular, in relation to rearing children, psychologists have made the most alarming mistakes by glorifying logic at the expense of intuitive or emotional reasoning. For example, Watson, an American psychologist of the early 1900s, told a generation of parents the following:

> Never hug and kiss them, never let them sit on your lap. If you must, kiss them once on the forehead when they say goodnight. Shake hands with them in the morning. Give them a pat on the head if they have made an extraordinary good job of a difficult task.[1]

This way of thinking was devoid of emotional reasoning, based on the purely logical idea that a logical response to children, rather than an emotional one, would teach them to be responsible human beings, able to control their emotions. Watson saw emotions as problematic. He even described love in terms devoid of emotion. He believed that a baby was conditioned to love its mother by being rewarded with mother's milk each time the baby was close to the mother. The idea that a child's love of its mother was nothing more than a learned response to receiving milk was debunked later, of course, but it is a perfect example of how logical reasoning and wisdom can be complete opposites. It is only when logical reasoning and emotional reasoning are combined that one can foster wisdom.

The emphasis on logic and devaluing of emotions led to institutional policies for children that were life threatening. As discussed in chapter 1, until the 1940s, institutions for children were places where children were not to be held or cuddled. Even though children had all of their physical needs met, some died because their emotional needs were not met. Despite the likely concerns of the people who worked with the children, the policies were kept in place. An emotional response to this situation would have been considered hysterical. Caregivers would have likely been accused of not being capable of being logical. Tragically, it has been assumed for years that if one is emotional, it is not possible to be logical and vice versa. The discounting of emotions has led to the belief that emotions need to be controlled with the mind and, interestingly, has resulted in the belief that the emotion and the behavioral expression of the emotion are one and the same.

This is partly due to how powerful emotions are. To truly experience an emotion is to experience something bigger than yourself. To choose your behavior when you are in the midst of something so powerful requires a deep respect for both the emotion and your own ability to choose your behavior in the face of it. Without the ability to choose one's behavior in the face of a powerful emotion, the emotion cannot be used as a guide. Without awareness and choice, emotions will instead become controlling forces in our lives, either consciously or unconsciously, rather than the guiding forces they should be.

How Emotions Take Over Your Life

An emotion can become unconscious if we try to control the emotion rather than the behavioral response to an emotion. Once an emotion is unconscious, we are unable to choose how to express it because we aren't aware we even feel it. It can take control of our lives at any moment. One common and striking example of this is when couples try not to be angry anymore with one another and stop being able to have an affectionate or physical relationship with each other. Trying not to feel one emotion seems to dampen all the emotions. Suppressing anger can also lead to depression, which can be viewed as an implosion of anger. It is a deadening or numbing of all feelings. Many people describe it as an experience of not being able to engage in one's own life. If you've ever been depressed, then you understand how difficult it is to choose your behavior when you feel depressed. The simplest of tasks seems to be impossible to accomplish.

All parents occasionally try to distract their children from their emotions, thinking that they are teaching their children how to cope with the emotions. However, distracting yourself from an emotion teaches you to pretend it's not there, not to cope with it. It may be a good temporary strategy; for example, if you are at work and cannot address the emotion fully or if you are with someone who will try to make you feel ashamed for expressing it in a healthy way, it's better to wait until you are in a safe place to fully experience that emotion.

Oftentimes, people confuse distraction from emotions with happiness. When you hear someone say, "I just wanted her to feel better" or "I was just trying to make her happy," usually they are talking about trying to distract someone from their pain to make them smile. It sounds harmless enough, but if we teach our children to cope this way, we may be setting them up for addiction. Essentially, addictions start as a way to distract us from emotional pain. Ironically, dealing with the pain you are trying to avoid is always easier than dealing with the consequences of trying to avoid the pain.

All Emotions Are Related to Our Desire for Personal Power

Experiencing emotions fully while choosing the behavioral response is truly the epitome of psychological health. To choose one's behavioral response to an intense emotional experience, though, requires us to be adept at emotional coping. The ability to tolerate the uncomfortable state of an emotion is central to being able to make the decision about how to respond to it.

Essentially, all emotions that are difficult to deal with begin with a feeling of powerlessness. Anger results from our trying to get control over feeling powerless. Think about the last time you were angry. For example, perhaps you were angry because you asked your child nicely several times to pick his shoes from the middle of the living room floor, but he kept playing video games instead. The expression that we call anger is actually often an attempt to get rid of the feeling of powerlessness. To be able to manage our anger, we have to learn how to cope with feeling powerless, so that we can be aware of what behavior is best to choose in the situation.

Sadness results from our giving up over feeling powerless. Fear results from anticipation of being powerless. Happiness results from letting go of the need for power. Temporary happiness results from getting what we want at the moment. Getting what we want allows us to let go of the need for power, but only temporarily. However, only by letting go of the need for power—or, in other words, having faith in our lives or in what happens or in a power greater than ourselves—do we live in a state of continuous happiness.

Emotions and Morality

Emotions can have a powerful physical effect on us. Our physiological response to an emotion can be as uncontrollable as the emotion itself. An intense emotion causes our pupils to dilate and our heart rate and rate of breathing to increase. It may also cause us to perspire, cry, or shake. Physiological responses are different from behavioral responses, because generally speaking, we have no control over them. An exception is people with antisocial personality disorder, more commonly known as psychopaths or sociopaths. Psychopaths have no physiological or emotional responses to things that would upset most people. For example, they can pass a lie detector test when they are lying.

That's because lie detectors measure the physiological responses the body has to intense emotion, such as guilt. Psychopaths can pass lie detector tests, because they don't feel guilty or get nervous when they lie. They are disconnected from their emotions. They can hurt or even kill other people without any emotional or physical response because they also have no conscience.

Most people don't understand that emotions are actually the basis of morality. Many times it is the ache in our hearts that motivates us to reach out to help someone who is hurting. To treat others compassionately or as you would wish to be treated requires empathy. Empathy requires an awareness and understanding of one's own feelings and the ability to recognize and connect with the emotions in others. Without emotional connection, empathy would not be possible and neither would compassion or morality.

Sitting With Emotions

To connect deeply with emotions and reveal the wisdom they have to offer requires us to "sit" with them, without reacting, without distracting ourselves from them, talking ourselves out of them, or suppressing them. This is, essentially, the definition of emotional coping; if practiced regularly, sitting with our emotions allows us to follow them to the depths of our being. Practicing sitting with emotions is actually an ancient spiritual practice,[2] and it is a practice at the heart of one of the most well-researched and successful psychological treatments for adults with personality disorders.[3] It is also what you have been practicing when you use a reflective response to your child's emotions. You are "being with" or "sitting with" your child in the emotions he or she is experiencing, instead of reacting to your urge to make them go away or unintentionally ask your child to suppress them. When you practice a reflective response, you are also sitting with the emotional pain or discomfort you feel when your child is hurting or angry. Being able to sit with your emotions, rather than react to them, allows you to focus on what your child needs and to choose the most appropriate behavior to meet your child's needs.

Teaching Instead of Punishing

As stated earlier, the epitome of psychological health is the ability to fully experience an emotion while choosing your behavior. It can also be defined as emotional maturity. To teach your child to do this requires that you, first, have an openness to his or her feelings and that you also have been practicing with reflective responding. The next step in promoting your child's emotional health and maturity is to teach him or her the appropriate behavioral expression of an emotion. Unfortunately, most of us have a tendency to punish our children for an inappropriate behavioral expression of an emotion rather than teaching the appropriate expression. Because of this, most adults don't know how to express emotions in a mature or healthy way. We either "stuff" them or explode, without understanding that there is a middle ground.

Most of the time parents punish children for being angry, misunderstanding that it is not the feeling that needs to be controlled, only the behavior. Punishing a child for feeling something teaches him to keep feelings to himself, to "stuff" his feelings, and to try and control those feelings. This practice not only disconnects our children from their feelings, it harms our relationship with our children because they are not able to open up to us about what they are feeling.

Most of us have also learned to set limits using shame and fear. This is actually trying to manipulate children into behaving appropriately by scaring them. For example, when you yell, threaten to take something away, or spank, that's using fear. When you say things like "What were you thinking?!" or "I can't believe you did that!" or "Now don't wait until the last minute again to start doing your homework and then come crying to me that you can't get it done!" you're using shame. Using shame to control children is so ingrained in most of us that we aren't even aware that we are doing it. I remember an incident at the grocery store in which this fact became very clear to me. Dylan is a drummer. I love the drums and I love to hear him play them; however, it did irritate me when he was beating on every available object, every minute of the day. I didn't realize how shaming I was being in asking him to stop until one day at the grocery store I said in a very irritated, disgusted tone, my eyes closed, my face tense and frowning, "Will you please, please stop that. It is driving me crazy!" When I opened my eyes, though, it wasn't Dylan I saw, it was a complete stranger who had been tapping on the counter. Imagine how differently it sounds to say those words, in that tone of voice, to a stranger. I was horrified and apologized immediately, explaining that I thought he was my son. I was also aware for the first time how disrespectful and shaming I had been when asking Dylan to stop drumming. Why was it all right to talk to my child in a way that would never be all right to use with someone else? I realized that many times I didn't set limits with my child or someone else because I didn't want to be disrespectful or shaming. Most of us are afraid to say "No" when we should because we don't know how to say it in a loving, respectful way.

Setting Limits With Love and Compassion

There are three easy steps to setting a limit in a respectful way. The first step is to acknowledge the feeling. For example, "Dylan, I know you love to drum." By acknowledging the feeling, you are communicating to the child that you understand him or her. Most of us are more willing to cooperate if we feel understood and cared for. You also want to communicate with this step that it's okay to feel any way you want to feel. Since feelings can't and shouldn't be controlled, you will focus on teaching your child to control the behavior, not the feeling.

The second step is to communicate the limit—for example, "…but the grocery store counter is not for drumming on." Stating the limit in this way eliminates the shame. You are telling the child in a very matter-of-fact way, "that's just not what that's for"; you aren't telling the child he's bad or annoying or not even that he shouldn't do it. The third step is to target the choice, to tell Dylan what he can do instead: "You can practice drumming when we get home." This is such an important step, because it's so important to teach children the appropriate behavior to use when expressing a feeling or desire.

This method is a therapeutic way of setting limits and is called ACT limit-setting[4] for *Acknowledge* the feeling, *Communicate* the limit, and *Target* the choice. Essentially when you use ACT, you are communicating to the child: "I understand how you feel. It's okay to feel that way, but you can't *act* that way when you feel like that. You can act this way when you feel like that." It is also important to communicate this message in a loving way, not an angry way.

Why It's Worth It

I learned to use ACT limit-setting when my daughter, Deva, was 3 years old. We were going through a time when mornings were very difficult, because Deva did not want to cooperate and would yell and say "No" a lot in a disrespectful tone. I decided to try ACT, saying, "Deva, I know you're angry, but I'm not for yelling at. You can tell me you're angry in a nice voice." It didn't faze her. In fact, she seemed even more determined to be hard to get along with. I spoke to Dr. Landreth the next day and asked him what to do. He suggested that I focus more on the empathy and make sure I really understood how she was feeling. I seriously doubted that Deva wasn't feeling anger and that I hadn't empathized enough, but I decided to take Dr. Landreth's advice anyway. The next morning as she was yelling and rebelling, it dawned on me that it wasn't really anger, it was that she wanted to boss me around because she felt bossed around. I used ACT again, this time saying, "Deva, I know you want to be the boss. You're tired of me telling you what to do and you want to tell me what to do, but I'm not for bossing around. If you want to boss someone around, you can line up your stuffed animals and boss them around." It worked like a charm. She couldn't wait to get ready, so she could go to her room and line her stuffed animals up and boss them around. Everywhere we went, for years, she would line things up—chairs, pillows, and toys—and tell them what to do. I was so happy that my daughter had found a way to express her need to be a leader and a teacher in a way that didn't irritate me or get her in trouble with other people. Not only that, she was easy to entertain wherever we were! I didn't truly understand, though, how much ACT would benefit her when I started to use it. She began to set limits in the same way. The first time I noticed it, she was talking to her brand new kitten. She said, "Tickles, I know you want to go outside, but you're too little to go outside. You can go outside when you're older." She didn't realize she was using ACT, that was just the way she was used to hearing limits set.

When Deva was only 8 years old, she taught me how valuable ACT limit-setting is. When I picked her up from school, I could see how angry she was before she got to the car. When she got into the car, she told me that she was really mad at the vice-principal of her school because he told the kids in the lunchroom to "Shut up!" We taught our children that it is disrespectful to say "Shut up" to anyone and had a rule against saying it (unless you were saying it in a joking way, like Stacy on *What Not to Wear*). "I can't believe the vice-principal of an elementary school would even think of saying such a thing to the whole lunchroom," she said. "Something needs to be done about it," she exclaimed. What my daughter didn't know about me is how terrified I was of elementary schools. When I was in the first grade, I had a teacher who would beat me for not making my letters as small as a typewriter. She was a miserable woman who wouldn't let the children in the classroom use the bathroom. I was lucky I never had an accident, but imagine the horror of watching your classmates having to empty their bladders at their desks, in front of the whole class. I was so afraid that I stopped drinking. Later that year, I was hospitalized for bladder problems, possibly due to being afraid to drink anything. My parents never knew about any of this until I was in my thirties. I didn't realize my teacher was being abusive. I had wonderful, loving parents who would have intervened had they known, but at 6 years old I believed that only "bad children" had problems in school and I wanted to be "good."

To this day, the scariest place on earth for me is an elementary school. I would rather be in a prison full of hardened criminals than at an elementary school. So when my daughter said something should be done, I panicked. I began to make excuses saying, "Well, honey, maybe he had a bad day. Everyone makes mistakes." Deva persisted though: "It doesn't matter if he had a bad day, he shouldn't have done that. He needs to be respectful, even if he's having a bad day." She was saying to me what I had said to her and she was right. "Well, okay, honey. I'll call him," I said. "No, Mom. I want to talk to him," Deva said, to my astonishment. "What do you want to say, honey?" I asked. She replied, "I want to tell him that I know he gets angry when kids are loud in the lunchroom, but that we're not for saying 'Shut up' to. That he can tell our teachers or take away our recess if we're loud, but that he shouldn't say 'Shut up.'" She was using ACT! At that moment, I realized how valuable ACT limit-setting is. My daughter knew how to say "No" in a respectful way. She could stick up for herself with someone in authority, in situations where most kids would be too afraid. Not only that, she had demonstrated that she believed it was important to take responsibility for one's behavior. She didn't say the kids should have no consequence, just that the consequence should be given in a respectful way. Not only had she demonstrated her ability to say "No" in a respectful way, she had implied in her solution that self-respect was more important to her than "getting off easy." While some kids would have preferred being treated disrespectfully to missing recess, Deva was saying the opposite.

I honestly had no idea that using ACT would result in such important benefits for my daughter. I was just doing what I thought was the right thing to do, but I was doing it without fully understanding what impact it would have. Setting limits with shame or fear may change behaviors, but it could never teach children to stick up for themselves in a respectful way, to take responsibility for their mistakes, or to realize the importance of self-respect.

When Deva walked into the school to talk to the vice-principal, he had already left, so she decided to leave a note saying almost exactly what she told me she would say to him if she had a chance to talk to him in person. So far as we know, he never said "Shut up" to the kids in the lunchroom again—at least, not when Deva was around.

Delaying Gratification and Increasing Frustration Tolerance

Using ACT limit-setting teaches children to cope with their emotions, to find an appropriate behavioral expression that doesn't suppress emotions or hurt themselves or others. It can also be used to teach children to delay gratification or wait for what they want. For example, if your child is complaining a lot and you don't have the energy to empathize anymore, you can say, "Johnnie, I know you're really mad at your sister for not wanting to play the things you want to play, but my ears can't listen right now. If you still need to talk about it, we can sit down at 7:15 tonight and you can tell me everything you want to say." If your child wants a toy when you're at the store and you don't want to buy it, you can say, "You love that toy and want it right now, but we're not spending any money on toys today. You can put it on your wish list for birthday or Christmas." If your child has meltdowns during homework time, you can say, "Susie, I know this homework is frustrating and you just feel like giving up, but homework time is the same as school time and the rules are the same as they would be for school. Homework time and school time are not time for giving up, they're time to learn how. If you're still upset about it and want to cry after we finish, you can do that then. Right now, though, you pretend you're at school and act like you would if I were your teacher and I'll pretend I'm the teacher." If your child is complaining about doing chores, you can say, "I know you don't want to do your chores and you don't think it's fair, but chore time is not negotiation time. If you want to talk about it after your chores are done, we can talk about it then." You probably realize that 90 percent of the time the problem is usually solved by the time you are ready to listen; however, be sure to tell your child, "Now it's time for me to listen about what you were trying to talk to me about earlier." If you don't follow through, your child won't be willing to cooperate later when you ask him or her to wait until 7:15 or after homework or chores.

Promoting Security

One of the most important functions of limit-setting is providing security for your child. The rule of thumb is,

☝ Where there are no limits, there is no security.[4]

When you use ACT, you are communicating to your child that you know how to handle any feeling or behavior he or she is struggling with in a loving way. When children don't have limits, they are basically taking care of themselves, because if parents don't set limits, the child is in control rather than the parent. When children act out in hurtful ways to others and no one intervenes, it hurts their self-image. They begin to see themselves as a problem or as a bad person.

As a therapist working with childhood abuse and trauma, I have found that both kids and adults test the limits before they reveal their deepest pain. It seems to be a way of expressing the message that "I won't let you see my pain until I know I can trust you to handle whatever I do in a loving and firm way." If you handle your children's acting out in a harsh and shaming way that hurts them or you just ignore the acting out, you are giving the message that you can't handle them.

Using ACT promotes your children's ability to trust you. When they have a problem, they learn that they can come to you to help them handle the situation because they know you will not shame them. Because ACT is focused on solutions rather than on punishment, it teaches your children that you are on their side, ready to face with them whatever mistakes they have made in a loving and caring way.

No One Can Do It All the Time

It's important to remember that no matter how hard you try, you can't always remember to use ACT. I write about or teach ACT every day and I still make the same mistakes you do sometimes. Luckily, my children know how to use ACT, too! "Mom, I know you're having a rough day, but I'm not for yelling at. You can tell me whatever you need to tell me in a respectful way." It's such a relief to know that in using ACT I have taught my kids to protect themselves, even from me, and to be resilient to the mistakes I will make as a parent.

If it's hard for you to remember to use ACT, you might be waiting until you're too frustrated to use it. Because ACT is therapeutic, you don't have to wait until you're at your wit's end to use it; you can use it any time you start to feel tense. You can use it with anyone in your life, not just your kids. For example, "Stan, I understand you want me to work late tonight, but I have to see my daughter's play. I can take some work home, or I can come in early tomorrow."

It's also important to realize that ACT does not always work in changing a behavior; sometimes a second line of defense, called "choice-giving," is needed. Choice-giving will be discussed in chapter 6. It's important to master ACT, though, before you learn choice-giving.

Guidelines for Expressing Difficult Emotions

Remember that when you're using ACT, you're teaching your child an appropriate expression of a difficult emotion. This is very hard at first because most of us didn't learn the appropriate expression of difficult emotions. To truly understand your child's emotions, you must first try to understand the world through your child's eyes as fully and completely as you can. Once you feel you have connected emotionally to what your child is experiencing, imagine what would be a satisfying yet appropriate expression. What might be satisfying for one child might not be for another. For example, for Dylan, the most satisfying way to express anger was to hit a punching bag we had hanging in the garage. For Deva, it was to write it in her journal. We learned this when she was in the third grade.

The third grade at my daughter's school was infamous for difficult teachers. In fact, there was a parent support group specifically for the third grade at her school because the teachers were so difficult to deal with. We addressed the situation early on, explaining to Deva that some people had said that the third-grade teachers were not always fair and that we would do whatever we could but that this would also give her an opportunity to learn how to cope with really difficult situations. At the time, she had her heart set on being the president of the United States, so we explained that she could think of this as part of her training, because the president has to deal with really difficult people in a diplomatic way. Come to think of it, this is probably what led to her interaction with the vice-principal.

When she would get in the car in the afternoons after a day in third grade, sometimes crying because of how shaming and disrespectful her teachers were, she would tell us what she wished she could say or do to her teachers. We explained to her that although she couldn't say it to her teachers' faces, she could write a story about doing whatever she wanted to do to her teachers or saying whatever she wanted to say. Interestingly, and certainly not coincidentally, she won a writing award in the fourth grade. She developed into an extraordinary writer because her writing is so engaging and emotional.

Your child's age is also important to consider. For example, it's very satisfying for a 3- or 4-year-old to hiss like a snake or growl like a lion when he or she is mad, but not for a 16-year-old. If you've tried your best and still can't come up with something satisfying, remember that learning how to cope is difficult. Tell your child, "I know you're upset and writing in your journal just doesn't feel like it will help, but yelling and screaming is not allowed in this part of the house. If you need to do that, you can yell and scream in your pillow, or if you need me to listen, I can do that at 7:15 this evening."

Sometimes children tend to express feelings inappropriately when they don't understand what they are feeling or when they are afraid of asking for what they need directly. For example, sometimes when children are exaggerating something or acting in an annoying way, they really want attention but are afraid to ask for it directly. You can say, "I know you want my attention right now, but you don't have to make things sound really bad to get my attention. You can just say, 'Mom, I need your attention right now.'" When Dylan was sick one day and had to stay in bed and miss a party, instead of throwing a fit or whining, he simply said, "Mom, I need you to 'poor-baby' me." To ask directly for what you need is exactly the opposite of being manipulative. Remember, if your children are being manipulative, it means they don't know how to ask, or are afraid to ask directly, for what they need.

To help your children express jealousy appropriately, you could say, "I know you're mad at Susie because I'm proud of her for making all As, and you're afraid I love her more because her grades are better, but I love you both no matter what grades you make. Susie is not for calling names, but if you feel afraid I won't love you as much, you can just tell me. Everybody feels that way sometimes. If you need to hear how much I love you and that I could never love anyone more than you, you can just ask me."

Practice ACT

When you practice ACT limit-setting, you are not trying to make your child stop feeling the way he or she does, you are teaching an appropriate behavioral expression of the emotion he or she is experiencing. The following scenarios give you an opportunity to practice teaching instead of punishing by using ACT. Remember to focus on what your child needs to learn for each of the following situations.

1. "There is no way I'm going to eat that for dinner. I want pizza."
2. "I can't do my chores. I'm sick to my stomach and I don't feel good."
3. "You shouldn't get to watch that movie if I can't."
4. "It's not fair if she gets a new pair of shoes and I don't."
5. "I'm not going to school this morning. I have a huge pimple on my nose and everyone will make fun of me."

6. "I should be able to go to the mall by myself. Everyone else does. You're just overprotective."
7. "I wouldn't have yelled at him if he hadn't yelled at me first."
8. "I don't think I should have to do the dishes. I hate doing them."

How did you respond to these statements? Some acceptable responses are described below.

ACT Answer Sheet

1. *There is no way I'm going to eat that for dinner. I want pizza.*

   "I know that pizza is your favorite food, but tonight we're having chicken and broccoli. You can have pizza when it's a special occasion." Don't think you have to be a short-order cook or give in to your child's demands for fast food. Remember that giving your children everything they want means they aren't getting what they need. Children don't always want what they need, so as parents it's important to make sure you're focused on their needs. Stating the limit in a calm and matter-of-fact way will send the message that you are serious and you can handle the situation.

2. *I can't do my chores. I'm sick to my stomach and I don't feel good.*

   "I know you aren't feeling well, but if you don't have a fever, it's important to do your work even when you don't feel good. After you're through, you can rest for a while." Sometimes kids say they feel bad just to get out of doing something they don't want to do. Sometimes, they can even convince themselves that they feel really bad if they don't want to do something. Instead of focusing on whether or not they feel bad, focus on what they need to learn for adulthood. When they are adults, it will be important for them to get their work done, even if they don't feel great. If your child has a chronic illness, this lesson becomes even more important, because you don't want her illness to completely take over her life.

3. *You shouldn't get to watch that movie if I can't.*

"You think that I should have the same rules you do, but I'm a grownup and I get to decide what is right for me. When you're a grownup, you will get to decide for yourself." Adults can do things that kids shouldn't do and kids need to know that. I've heard parents justify letting their kids see R-rated movies, explaining, "Oh, it's okay, he knows it's not real." Have you ever been to a scary movie and not been able to sleep with the light off because you were so scared? You knew the movie wasn't real, but it didn't stop you from being scared. The research shows that violence in movies affects adults and children, leading not just to aggressive behavior but also to depression. It's not worth the risk.

4. *It's not fair if she gets a new pair of shoes and I don't.*

"I know you want a new pair of shoes too, but your shoes are still in good shape. When your shoes are worn out, you can have a new pair." No matter what anyone says, you do not have to do something for one child just because you do it for another child. That would be like saying, "Well, we put a cast on Johnny's arm, so now we have to put a cast on everyone's arm." To be fair does not mean to get everyone the same thing, it means to make sure everyone gets what he or she needs.

5. *I'm not going to school this morning. I have a huge pimple on my nose and everyone will make fun of me.*

"I know you're worried about what everyone will think, but it's time to go to school. You can talk to me about your day when you get home." There is so much pressure on kids socially that it can sometimes be overwhelming, but letting kids stay home from school because of social pressures doesn't help them learn to cope with the pressure. Remember that your focus is on teaching your children to cope with the difficulties of life, not protect them from them.

6. *I should be able to go to the mall by myself. Everyone else does. You're just overprotective.*

"I know you feel like I'm overprotective, but I'm the adult and I make the rules for now. When you're an adult, you will get to make those decisions." Sometimes it's difficult to know what the boundaries should be for your child, especially during the teenage years. There isn't an easy answer, but remember when you don't get it right, you're still teaching them how to build coping skills!

7. *I wouldn't have yelled at him if he hadn't yelled at me first.*

"It's hard to react respectfully when someone is being disrespectful to you, but even though he yelled at you first, it's important to treat him respectfully. If he's yelling you can tell him in a respectful way to stop yelling." All of us try to justify our mistakes by blaming our behavior on others. It's important to let your children know that they are accountable for their own behavior, regardless of the situation.

8. *I don't think I should have to do the dishes. I hate doing them.*

"I know you don't want to do those right now, but chore time is not negotiation time. When you get through doing your chores, we can talk about your concerns." Don't be drawn into dramatic situations when it's time to do chores or homework. Set a time aside for when chores and homework dramas can be discussed later. If your child's attitude about chores or homework is a problem, you can set a limit on that too, by saying, "I know you don't like to do the dishes, but it's important to have a good attitude when you work. If you're angry about having to do the dishes, you can complain to me tonight at 7:15."

Review of Previous Homework

You've completed your first play session! Did the time during the session go by quickly? If so, that means you're enjoying and absorbed in the session. If you're feeling discouraged about your progress or the level of mastery of skills when you review your tape, you are probably being too critical of yourself. Don't forget to focus on what you did well in the play session. What skills come easily for you? What do's and don'ts have you already mastered? As you continue to view and evaluate your sessions, set small, realistic goals—and remember: your play session doesn't have to be perfect. I've been having special playtime for years and I've never had a perfect session.

Homework[4]

1. Have another play session this week and evaluate your tape of it using the evaluation form.
2. Continue to reflect your child's feelings
3. Set limits with your child using ACT this week.

5

YOUR CHILD'S PLACE IN YOUR HEART

Survival Tip 5

Be Fascinated

After weeks of filial therapy training a client asked me, "When will I get to the bottom of this?" When I asked her what she meant, she explained, "When will we figure out why my child is so defiant?" She had been thinking that the reason my son stopped being defiant when I had done filial therapy with him was because we found out about his dyslexia and she was hoping all along to find out what was blocking her child. I explained that it wasn't the dyslexia that was causing Dylan to act the way he did, it was our relationship. It is always the relationship that needs to be the focus when a child is behaving destructively or inappropriately. Even if your child has a diagnosis that includes symptoms that no amount of love, understanding, correction, or treatment can heal, it will come down to learning how to relate in a loving way to your child just the way he is. The child is never the problem. The problem is always figuring out how to relate to your child in a way that meets his or her needs (not necessarily wants) at the deepest possible level.

👍 Keep your eye on the doughnut and not on the hole.[1]

As parents we often get caught up in what's wrong with our child, his shortcomings or faults, especially if we have the same ones! We forget to focus on the beautiful, loving, playful qualities our child has. Practice letting go of the problem you are having with your child by focusing on the joy he brings you. This is very different from trying to make yourself feel good or pretending you feel good when you don't. You can acknowledge your worry about the problem and then choose to focus instead on the joy that your child brings you. Simply make the decision to start taking notice of the moments when your child brings you joy. They don't have to be big things. It can be the little curl of hair on his forehead, her sweet smile, the way he holds a flower, the way she says "snissors" instead of scissors, how small and precious his feet and hands are, how she reaches for you, how he runs to you when you come home, how round her cheeks are, how lyrical his laugh, how curious she is, how hard he tries. The list is endless. There is so much joy in parenting your child that you may not be focusing on. You may even want to keep a notebook to help make you be more aware of the joy that your child brings you.

Beyond Dysfunction

It's extremely difficult for us to be aware of the dysfunctional patterns in our relationships. A friend of mine recovering from alcoholism once told me it was like trying to read the label of the bottle from the inside of the bottle. Her alcoholism was obvious to everyone but her. To understand her dysfunctional behaviors required her to adopt a completely different perspective.

The dysfunctional things you do in your relationship with your child have been handed down to you from generations of your family; to let yourself see them is to cut through generations of complex defenses. Regardless of who you are, the dysfunctional patterns are there. We all have dysfunctional ways of relating to others, myself included. Psychologists aren't free from dysfunction, but their training helps them to be able to be aware of their dysfunctional ways of relating so that they don't interfere with therapy. That is the purpose of teaching you how to be therapeutic with your children: so that they have at least

30 minutes every week with you completely free of any dysfunctional behaviors.

By practicing freedom from dysfunction every week for 30 minutes once a week you are learning a new way of being with your child. During those 30 minutes you are giving up being right, giving up your need to control your child, and letting go of the problems in your relationship. It's a very brave and difficult thing for anyone to do, because essentially all of our dysfunction is related to our desire for personal power, to have things the way we want them, to find comfort, to feel that we matter. In fact, the only real addiction is to our desire for personal power, and we are all addicts in this sense. To let go of these desires and adopt instead an openness to what is present—and a flexibility to working with it—is, at first, very threatening.

Practicing Fascination

What allows the dysfunctional patterns to change in the play session is the parent's attitude of fascination. Instead of being in control, we are filled with wonder as we watch our children's psyche unfold. The sessions provide a time for discovery of who your child is on the deepest possible level. The practice of the play session is to learn how to stop reacting to the urges and feelings you have when you are with your child. You take time to observe your urges and emotional reactions so that you, too, unfold before yourself. You sit with and question your reactions with the same fascination and curiosity that you allow yourself to have about your child. As you do, you begin to understand why you feel the way you do and why you react the way you do.

Review the Videotapes

Set the Stage for a Structured Play Session

Reviewing your videotapes is one of the most important steps in learning how to create an environment free from dysfunction.

As you watch your tape, grade yourself with the skills checklist provided in chapter 3. The first thing to evaluate is whether or not you "set the stage."

As I was reviewing a tape of a father doing his first play session with his daughter, I noticed that he hadn't arranged the toys; instead, he had left them in the box and in their packages. When I asked him about it, he insisted that he just hadn't had the time. Regardless of the situation, not having enough time will never be the real reason you don't do something. Perhaps you can say you didn't make it a priority, but as I've said before, you certainly have 30 minutes once a week. The question becomes "Why didn't you make this a priority?" Remember to practice fascination with yourself. Ask yourself this question in a curious way, rather than in a shaming way. You're not a bad person; you are avoiding this detail for some reason. You just have to figure out why. As the tape continued, the father's reasons became clear. As his daughter struggled to open the packages, she gave up several times and asked for help. In studying the father's feelings during these exchanges, he was able to realize that he felt that his role as a father was to come to his daughter's rescue. He was able to see how he constantly created situations for his daughter in which she would need him to come to her rescue. Later, we discovered the underlying issue the father had was related to a wish he developed as a child and held onto all of his life for his own father to come to his rescue. All of this came to light as he uncovered layer after layer of his emotions as he watched the sessions. Eventually, as he grieved, understanding that his wish was not going to come true, he was able to see how empowering his daughter was more important than rescuing her.

Body Language

Three categories in the skills checklist associated with body language include leaning forward, being relaxed and comfortable, and appearing interested. If you're not able to do these, you need to ask yourself, "Why?"

Many times when parents have trouble conveying interest and comfort in a session it is because they are wrapped up in something that happened before the session or in an emotion they are having trouble coping with. For example, as I was watching a father's play session with his son, I realized that his body language was tense. Although he was reflecting feelings, tracking, and avoiding asking questions while his son danced around the room making jokes about bodily functions, his arms were crossed and his body was not turned toward his child. When I stopped the tape to ask him how he was feeling at that moment during the session, he explained, "I was angry because he was doing the same thing during the session that he got into trouble for at school."

There is no question that what he was doing would be inappropriate at school, but this was special playtime, a time to work out behavior problems. The best way for a child to work out those problems is to bring them to an accepting environment where they can be understood. In effect, the father was communicating to his son that he did not want him to bring his problems to the play session. As the father put aside his own feelings and focused on his son's feelings, he began to reflect how humiliated the son felt. His body language communicated the acceptance and openness he allowed himself to feel in his heart. As the sessions evolved and the father was able to let the son's message unfold, the son eventually revealed that he had been upset with his father for not standing up to his wife (the boy's stepmother) when she humiliated him. The father realized that he had become too passive in his marriage, trying very hard not to be like his own father, who had been abusive to his mother. The father began to shift the family system by setting limits with his wife in a loving but firm way (using ACT), rather than the way his father had set limits with his mother. The son had stopped getting into trouble at school long before his behavior was understood or before the system changed, though, because his father had made a safe place for his message to be heard and understood.

Lean Forward and Appear Interested

Sometimes it's more difficult to understand why we can't appear interested in, and accepting of, our child's play. For example, as I watched a mother play with her son, I noticed that while she would keep making the effort to lean forward and appear interested in her son's play, she kept getting distracted by other toys or things in the room. She explained that she couldn't focus on her son because she had severe attention deficit/hyperactivity disorder (ADHD). However, there seemed to be more to the story because she could not identify her feelings when I asked her, "How are you feeling during the session at that point?" What became apparent after struggling several times to figure out how she was feeling was that she was very afraid of her feelings and *that*, in fact, was what had been distracting her, not just from her son's play but from everything important in her life as well. As she learned to focus on her feelings during sessions, she was gradually able to put them aside. What I learned from this client is that you have to acknowledge your own feelings in order to prevent them from interfering with the session.

Allow the Child to Lead

As you watch your tape, pay special attention to any time you lead the session. Most parents have difficulty noticing when they lead, but if you ask a question or make a suggestion, you're leading. It is easy to review your tape for this mistake. Just stop whenever you have asked a question and be fascinated with yourself; examine your intention. Ask yourself what you were feeling or what you were wishing would happen when you asked the question.

For example, while watching a tape with a recently divorced mother, I noticed that she started to ask questions during her session. Her daughter had taken the dolls and was acting out going back and forth between her mother's and father's houses. Her father had left her mother for someone else and his new girlfriend lived with him. In the play scene the little girl called the father's new girlfriend "Mommy." The mother asked, "How can that one be Mommy, if the other one is Mommy?" She went on to explain that there could only be one mommy. I stopped the tape and asked the mother what she was feeling when she asked her daughter about the other mommy. As she explained, she began to cry. She felt as though this woman had stolen her husband and was now stealing her children. She began to grieve the loss of her husband, her marriage, her sense of security, and the dreams she had for their future together.

By allowing your children the freedom to truly express their feelings, thoughts, and desires in special playtime, you may come face to face with painful feelings of your own. The feelings this mother had to deal with when hearing her daughter call her ex-husband's girlfriend "Mommy" were indeed excruciating. It's important, though, not to let those feelings interfere with the child's healing. In the example above, what the child needed was to feel secure and connected in both households. She also needed to know that her mother could put her own needs aside to focus on her daughter's needs. If the mother had continued to focus on avoiding her own emotional pain during sessions, she would have given her daughter the message that she could not discuss how she felt about her father or his new girlfriend or worse, that if she loved her father and his new girlfriend, she was hurting her mother.

Sometimes you may be tempted to excuse a question because you simply let the tone of your voice go up at the end of a perfectly good statement to make it into a question. These types of questions are still questions, though, and can definitely be leading.

Recently, a single father was showing me a tape of a play session with his daughter. The daughter had wanted to play hangman but then apparently became bored or interested in something else and wanted to stop playing hangman. The father responded, "You want to quit?" The tone of voice he used clearly communicated to his daughter the disappointment he was feeling and that it was not okay to quit. By the time he had recognized that he had led the session and tried to correct himself by saying "You can quit if you want to" in a very unconvincing tone, his daughter had gotten the message that she wasn't supposed to quit and pretended that she had never wanted to stop playing. When I asked the father what had happened to him during the session when he felt compelled to lead, he responded, "Winners never quit and quitters never win." I reflected that something about that was very important to him and he began to weep, explaining that his parents had been quitters, giving up on each other and giving up on him. His own unresolved pain from his childhood had made it difficult for him to let his daughter lead the session. He had been neglected and abused as a child, living on his own from the age of 15. He had survived a very difficult life by telling himself to never, ever give up. As we spoke, though, he began to realize that this mantra had allowed him to survive, but it had also made it impossible for him to let go when he needed to. He also realized that the real reason his parents couldn't connect emotionally with each other or with him at times was not because they gave up but because they couldn't let go—let go of anger, resentment, or the way they thought things should be. This realization seemed to transform him. He began to be willing to let go of anger and resentment and to practice compassion in all areas of his life, even in the most difficult relationships. He understood that he had not allowed himself to act compassionately before, because he had come to believe that it put him at risk, while acting angrily protected him. As he thought it through in session, though, he realized that the anger he had been using to protect himself had only hurt him. It had harmed the relationships that were most important to him and had made his life more difficult.

Another seemingly innocent way parents may lead the session is by making suggestions. Many times parents don't realize when they are making suggestions. You have to really look for them on your videotape. Be careful never to dismiss a suggestion for any reason. While it might not make a difference in every situation, you never know when your suggestion may interfere with your child's unfolding.

I remember a tape in which a father was having a play session with his little girl. She explained to the father that she was the baby and he was supposed to give her the baby bottle. He responded by saying, "Okay, I'll hold you and feed you the bottle." As he held her, he began talking sweetly to her as he did when she was a little baby. When I asked him to tell me what he was feeling at that moment, he explained that he was trying to be therapeutic. He wanted to heal his daughter and felt responsible for the pain she had suffered in their relationship. He realized as he spoke that he had been working on his issues, though, not his daughter's. As we pushed the play button to watch what happened next, the impact of his interference became obvious. His daughter quickly switched to a different play, one in which she was in control. She continued to play games that kept her in a winning mode for the rest of the session, so that she wouldn't have to take on the burden of her father's guilt.

Returning Responsibility

Another way children hide their true feelings from us is by trying to make us take over the lead in play sessions. It is common for children to ask for assistance or help when they don't really need it. Many times adults confuse loving with doing things for someone that he could have done for himself. Remember, though, that loving someone means focusing on what he or she needs. It's probably rare that what we need is for someone to do something for us that we can do for ourselves. Children, in particular, need to know that they are competent, capable, and persistent in the face of frustration more than they need to know that you will pamper or rescue them.

During the play session when you are focusing on how much you love and appreciate your child, you may be tempted to fall into old patterns of doing things for her that she can do for herself. It's natural that when we are feeling loving we want to cooperate and do whatever someone asks of us.

A mother I was working with had a great deal of trouble with this issue during play sessions with her daughter. She brought her 8-year-old daughter in because she was wetting herself during the day. During the play sessions her daughter would ask in the sweetest little voice, "Mommy, will you do it?" Regardless of how often we went over the appropriate response ("That's something you can do"), the mother would do whatever the child asked. In exploring the issue further, she realized that she believed that loving someone meant doing whatever that person asks you to do with a cheerful attitude. In viewing the tapes, she also realized that her daughter was trying very hard to show her mother love by asking her to do things she could do for herself. The mother remembered being a little girl and doing the same thing for her own mother, who was unable to take care of her due to severe mental illness. She would think up things her mother could do for her so that her mother would feel like she was a good mother. She realized she had passed down this same pattern to her child. She was not focusing on her daughter's needs; her daughter was focusing on making her mother feel good and was sacrificing her own needs.

After the mother realized that saying "That's something you can do" in a loving way was what her daughter really needed from her, the little girl was finally liberated from focusing on making her mother feel good all the time and began to focus on what she needed to grow and thrive. The relationship became more challenging for the mother, because for the first time in her life, the little girl began testing limits and showing anger. The wetting accidents finally stopped once the little girl believed that her mother could take care of her.

Tracking

Whenever the relationship with your child is challenging, there is something in the challenge that holds an important lesson. I worked with a curious father who was particularly frustrated by not being able to ask questions during the play session. His son seemed stuck in the play, repeating the same scene of a baby surrounded by army men over and over. Initially, he had asked questions, but whenever he did, his son would shut down. As the father and I viewed a tape of his son's play session, we both noticed that he had stopped asking questions and had become quiet and withdrawn. When I stopped the tape to ask him what he was feeling, he explained that he was bored and feeling trapped because he had to stop himself from being curious about his child's play, because it led him to ask questions. When I asked him to tell me what he was curious about he became very animated, asking many questions about his child's play, such as: "Why did he surround the baby with the army men? What does that mean? Where are the parents of the baby? Does he think he can't ask us for help when he needs it?" The father revealed in his questions that he was feeling anxious and guilty about his son's play. This is a common response. All parents worry about how their child might be hurting. The father learned, though, that by focusing on *tracking* whenever he felt as though he wanted to ask a question helped him to be led by his curiosity, rather than his guilt. For example, by simply observing what he was seeing and describing it ("I see the baby is surrounded by all those people")—or, in other words, tracking—he was able to give his curiosity a voice. He also learned to make statements about his curiosity that were not in question form, such as "I wonder what those people are doing around the baby." If his child didn't answer, he could simply track again by saying, "Hmm, I notice you didn't say anything about that. Maybe you don't want to talk about that right now." Eventually, the father was able to understand that he was so afraid about what his son might be feeling or dealing with that he hadn't been open to hearing what it was. As he was viewing the tape of his son's familiar scene, he understood how threatening the situation was for the baby in the play. When he thought about how this might apply to his son's situation, he began to cry. He immediately realized that his son, like himself, had felt very threatened by his father's anger and criticism. During the next session he reflected those feelings saying, "That baby must feel really scared with all those guns pointing at him. Maybe you feel that way sometimes when I get really angry." The boy looked up at his father in amazement and relief, understanding that his father was ready to help him with his struggles. After that session, the boy's play changed and so did his relationship with his father.

Tracking is particularly important to use when you are allowing yourself to feel fascinated by your child's play. Being guided by your own curiosity about your child's play will help you to master the skill of tracking because you will simply observe and describe those things about your child's play that fascinate you. Being fascinated also allows you to let go of what you may fear so that you can face it head on. If your child is stuck in play, repeating the same scene over and over, ask yourself if you are ready to really understand and face your child's pain.

Reflective Responding

As you watch your video, see if you can identify any feelings in your child that you didn't reflect during the session. In fact, this step is so important that I would recommend watching your tape a second time with just this exercise in mind. You can also pay attention to how you could reflect your child's feeling more sincerely or on a deeper level. The mastering of this skill is like any other: it comes with lots of practice. If you consistently forget to reflect feelings, it may be a clue about what you need to do in your relationship with your child. For example, as I was reviewing a tape with a foster mother, I realized that whenever her foster son began to play out scenes with the toys in which the boy's parents were being abusive, she became very quiet and when she did talk, she only tracked the behavior. She appeared to be very disconnected during the sessions whenever the boy's parents were in a play scene. When I asked her, "What are you feeling when he plays that out?" she explained that she was afraid she might damage her foster son in some way if she said the wrong thing. She explained that she did not want her foster son to go back to live with his biological parents. Her fear of her own feelings was preventing her from connecting with the child's feelings. She noticed when watching the sessions that her foster son had been playing out the abuse he had suffered with his mother and father and that she had not acknowledged it. Her tendency to ignore, rather than acknowledge, her son's feelings had led him to shut down and become bored during the session. Before the session was over, he was asking if he could leave. He became uninterested in the toys and in playing with her.

With this information in mind, she was able to put aside her feelings and be with her foster son in his. As he acted out the way he had been harmed in a play scene, the foster mother reflected, "The little boy is really scared. He doesn't understand what he did wrong." As the foster mother reflected the boy's pain, the play scene changed and the boy was given a "wise old owl" who cared for him and showed him love and compassion. Eventually, the little boy was able to talk about what had happened to him.

In the above situation and in the one following, the abuse that was being played out was already known by the parents. If you are playing with your child and suspect abuse is being played out that you don't know about, it's extremely important to take your child to a qualified professional to assess your child. It's possible to do more harm than good by asking leading questions. I have often had the experience in working with abused children that once they feel safe in a relationship, they will bring up abuse that hasn't been disclosed to anyone before. Again, if your child discloses abuse, it's important not to take on these issues all by yourself. While filial therapy has been proven effective with children who have been abused, it's an overwhelming issue that anyone would need help with.

Seeing the World Through Your Child's Eyes

When you are open to seeing the world through your child's eyes, you will feel connected with your child. As a beginning therapist working with children who had been abused or neglected, I found myself in a situation in which I had trouble feeling connected with a little boy named William. I was aware that, since I had been seeing William, I had not been making contact with him. I also began to have feelings of anger toward William's mother. Whenever William made progress, she became more and more difficult, usually sabotaging his progress. I believed at the time that it was my anger toward his mother that came between us and that in order to connect with him, I would have to push that anger aside. I began each session trying to talk myself out of the anger I felt, but our relationship still seemed shallow. Whenever I had had difficulty connecting with a child in the past, I used a simple technique where I imagined what the child saw, heard, and felt. For example, if a child was sitting on the carpet playing with a doll, I imagined the softness of the carpet on my knees, the cold vinyl of the doll in my hands, the perspective of sitting on the floor. In this way, I usually began to be pulled into the world of the child and then gradually began to understand the child's feelings and desires. For some reason, though, I could not enter into William's world.

During one session, I finally decided to get down on the floor with William so that I could actually see the toys as he did. I decided to be a child with him and indulge my desires to touch the toys and ask questions when I didn't understand the "game" he was playing. I also allowed myself to feel the resentment I felt toward his mother for sabotaging the work we had done. Then I began to understand that this dollhouse was a place where William wished he could live. I commented that he might be wishing he could run away to a house like the one he was playing with. A kind of strange, short, loud laugh burst out of him. I had never heard him make a sound like that before. It sounded like pent-up glee that had escaped from deep inside him, accidentally. In his play he reacted as though he had suddenly been freed. As he was putting the furniture in the dollhouse, I wondered out loud which one was him ("I wonder which one of those is you."), referring to the boy dolls in the box. He chose two dolls—one black haired, one blonde haired—and held them up. I said, "Those two are you." He seemed satisfied and gently tucked them into their bunk beds. After he had arranged the rooms with all the things he needed, he began to put together a plant, something he had never done before. It seemed to reflect the growth he was experiencing. He seemed to be forming a larger vision of himself and of the world. Later, I wondered out loud where the father doll would sleep ("I wonder where the father will sleep.") and he said, "Outside! Outside in the cold, until he learns his lesson." The gleeful noises exploded out of him again. He replied the same way when I wondered about the mother doll. I was sad for him, realizing that he had been put "out in the cold" all his life. It was so touching to see that he had built a place for himself where he had everything he needed. It felt good to know that, at least in some realm of existence, he really did have everything he needed. William seemed to make contact with some part of himself.

Our relationship changed dramatically. I realized that I had been having difficulty connecting with William because I didn't believe he could heal in the relationship he had with his mother. Those feelings in me became expressed as being very guarded and protective with William. I was afraid of the resentment I felt toward his mother, and I was afraid of damaging him in some way. I could only see his wound and his powerlessness. After this session with him, though, I was able to see a more complete picture of William. I was aware of his abilities to heal and his unlimited powers of imagination. I knew that no matter what he encountered, he had within him the ability to use the experience to deepen his life, as long as he was able to remain imaginative and connected to others. I also began to have a sense of what he might need in the dollhouse. That day I added two new figures, a ghost and a burglar, hoping that these images would awaken something within him that he needed and bring to him, at least in his imagination, the nurturing adults he needed in his life. Interestingly, during his next session, without my pointing out either new figure, William moved the ghost into the attic. The ghost protected and helped the boys and the burglar took off his mask to reveal his good side to William. "He's not really a bad guy. The mask just made him look that way," he explained. He then asked me if "they" made any fairy godfathers. I told him I had been looking for a wizard when I found the other figures and that I had seen a fairy godmother. He was very interested in both. I then told him that he didn't have to wait for me to buy them, because he could chose any doll he wanted to be the fairy godfather. He decided not to, but later he told me, "I love this so much. I wish I could take it home with me." The home he had always needed and hoped for had come alive for him.

Something else I learned from working with William is that forgiveness is a gift. It's not something we can make ourselves feel in our hearts. Of course, I can act in a forgiving and compassionate way, but until I feel it in my heart, I will not be able to forgive. Unfortunately, my feelings for William's mother have not changed much over the years and I hadn't really realized it until I started writing about William.

As I started looking over the paper about William that I had written for Dr. Landreth 14 years ago, to put his story in this book, I noticed a comment in the margins. Dr. Landreth had written, "You need more about the mother." I glanced over the sections of the paper, noting the information about the mother. The original paper was 20 pages long, so there was a lot of information I haven't included in this book. (The mother's diagnosis, functioning in all areas, appearance, behavior, and so forth, and all of the clinical information was there.) What was missing? It hit me suddenly: it was the compassion that was missing. I hadn't felt compassion for the mother. After 14 years, I had finally understood what Dr. Garry Landreth had wanted me to see. The most amazing thing about this, though, was that he hadn't said, "Theresa, you need to find compassion in your heart for this client's mother." He had simply said that I needed to write more about the mother, knowing that if I struggled to understand her, I would find compassion for her. Imagine for a moment how much faith you must have in other human beings to make a statement such as that without any more guidance than that, without having to make them see what you think is best, to give them the space to have their own epiphany.

This incident brings to mind another experience I had with Garry. I was talking with him about a client and told him, "Garry, this is the first client I ever haven't liked. I never remember not liking a client before and I don't know what to do!" He simply said, "Theresa, is it that you don't like them or is it that you're angry at them?" I thought for a moment and said, "No, I just really don't like them." "Hmmm," he said, nodding his head looking at me in such a way that I knew I had missed something, "Give yourself some time to think about it some more. Maybe you've missed something." He knew that I was just angry at my client, because he knew that whenever someone says "I don't like this person" he or she is really saying "I'm angry at this person." He also knows that whenever someone says "I am angry at this person," he or she is saying "I can't feel compassion for this person because I can't feel compassion for myself in this same area." Instead of telling me any of that, though, instead of giving me the answers, he let me figure them out. He had enough faith in me, in human nature, in innate wisdom, in the way the world is, to let me figure it out for myself.

Matching and Mirroring

One way to practice having faith in your child's innate wisdom is to match and mirror her tone of voice and play during the play session. I learned how valuable this exercise was from a mother who was very anxious about how her daughter had been affected by her recent divorce from her third husband, the girl's second stepfather. As the girl played out or drew pictures depicting the anger or sadness she felt about losing another father figure, the mother would reflect in a cheerful tone, "You feel sad!" At the time I thought the mother was just proud that she had remembered to reflect the feeling, rather than talk her daughter out of it; but as the mother practiced matching her daughter's tone while watching the tape, she began to realize that her cheerful tone protected her from empathizing with her daughter. As she began to empathize, she realized how difficult it was for her to experience the feelings without trying to rescue or fix her daughter's feelings to try and make her feel better. Matching the tone of her daughter's feelings and play without fixing or rescuing taught this mother how to have faith in her daughter and led to her creating a relationship in which her daughter could open up and talk to her about her feelings.

👍   Don't try to change everything at once.[1]

As you stop yourself from trying to shape or mold your child during the play sessions, you allow acceptance of who your child is. This acceptance is what allows you to relate to and harmonize with your child. The chaos we often feel in relationships is in our inability to make someone into whom we believe they should be or the inability to make ourselves into whom we believe we should be. If there is any limit to be set, it is only on the behavioral expression, not the feelings, thoughts, or ideas. As you might have noticed in the above examples, in order to give your child unconditional acceptance and compassion, you have to be willing to give it to yourself, also. Simply put, whenever we are being compassionate, we are not being dysfunctional. Chapter 8 will describe the three conditions for compassion.

Review of Previous Homework

You've had your second play session and have evaluated your skills. You've also practiced ACT limit-setting this week. Most parents are amazed at how well the ACT limit-setting works with their child. If you aren't getting results, try focusing more on seeing the world through your child's eyes and saying the limit in a loving, but firm way. There is also another step to limit-setting that will be discussed in the next chapter. Remember, you can practice special playtime skills anytime. The next time you're at the grocery store with your child and she is being difficult, practice the special playtime skills.

Homework[1]

1. Practice fascination during your play session this week and evaluate your session using the evaluation form and the "do's and don'ts" list.
2. Practice fascination whenever your buttons are pushed.
3. Make a "Doughnut Journal" to write down the moments of joy your child brings you.
4. Continue to reflect feelings and use ACT. The more you use these skills in the heat of the moment, the more harmony you will create.

6

GAINING YOUR
CHILD'S RESPECT

Survival Tip 6

Don't Be Responsible for
Things Your Child Can
Be Responsible For

Whether you realize it or not, this is the chapter you've been waiting for. You are finally going to learn the next step in limit-setting, called *choice-giving*.[1] I'm sure you've done some version of choice-giving, but you might have left out one of the steps that make it work. Choice-giving has been likened to a magic potion by parents, because it is so effective in changing their children's and their own behavior. Like any magic potion, though, you have to stick to the recipe or it won't work. Remember those cartoons where the wizard would substitute a frog's ear for a toad's hair and would get something he didn't bargain for? Choice-giving is the same way. You must follow the rules of choice-giving exactly or it won't work. Finish the entire chapter, practice the exercises, and give your child a choice a week for four weeks before you decide if it works or not.

Dr. Garry Landreth is responsible for developing the choice-giving technique. I highly recommend his video entitled *Choices, Cookies and Kids*,[1] which describes the technique. It can be purchased at specialplaytime.com. In the video he tells a story about his daughters fighting in the car on the way home. It's a story

we all know, because some version of it has happened to all of
us. His daughters are screaming and pushing each other in the
backseat of the car and it makes it very difficult to concentrate
on driving. He pulls over and is extremely frustrated. Incred-
ibly, this gentle, Mr. Roger's-like man, who has dedicated his
life to making the world a safer place for children, admits that
he thought about spanking his children! Think about that for a
moment. If that thought can cross his mind, it can cross anyone's
mind. We have all had similar thoughts, but we haven't acted
on those thoughts. Dr. Landreth describes himself as having an
intervening thought, which was,

> Yes, Garry, you could control them, but what would they have
> learned? They would have learned, "Go ahead and get as out of
> control as you want. You don't have to stop yourself—Dad will
> stop you," and I realized, I don't want that for my daughters.

This is such an important realization: by trying to control our
children, we teach them that they don't have to have self-control.
As explained in chapter 4, when you use shame or fear, you are
controlling your kids instead of teaching them self-control. If
you want your children to learn self-control, you have to give
them responsibility for their own behavior.

Dr. Landreth put the responsibility for his daughters' behavior in their hands by calmly explaining:

> We are instituting a new and significant policy within the con-
> fines of this automobile, and the policy is: If you choose to fight
> in the car on the way home, you choose not to get to watch TV
> tonight. If you choose not to fight in the car on the way home, you
> choose to get to watch TV. Which do you choose?

Before you say, "Oh, I've tried that and it doesn't work," consider
that saying "If you don't stop fighting, you don't get to watch
TV" is not the same. In fact, it is a threat, an attempt to use fear
to control your child's behavior. To use choice-giving requires

you to use the word *choose* four times so that it's clear where the responsibility lies. It also requires you to say it in a calm voice, not an angry one, because using an angry voice scares kids into changing their behavior. The idea is that your child should learn to control her own behavior not out of fear but out of her own choice to behave appropriately.

The rest of the story is also very important, because it shows the difference between failure and success in using this technique. As Dr. Landreth and his girls got back on the road to go home, his girls were quiet but after a few minutes they started fighting again. Dr. Landreth simply said in a calm voice, "I see you've chosen not to get to watch TV," and the girls were quiet again, all the way home—and it was a long way home. You know exactly what his girls said as they pulled into the driveway: "Do we get to watch TV?" They had been quiet all of the way home after Dr. Landreth had remarked on their choice. Should they be rewarded for good behavior? This is where most parents would allow their children to watch TV, but that would communicate to children that you don't really have to be responsible for your behavior or exercise self-control. In the short-term, it would, of course be easier to say, "Okay, you girls were good most of the way, go ahead and turn on the TV." That's not what Dr. Landreth did, though. He said, "I know you want to watch TV, but girls, the moment you chose to fight in the car on the way home, you chose to give up TV for the day." You probably know his girls' reaction. They "cried loudly as if the world was coming to an end." Isn't that what your child would do? I often hear parents tell me that they can't enforce the limits or choices that their children make because their children get too upset. It's okay for your children to get upset, though, as long as you are focused on what they need. Your children don't always want what they need and will get upset when you try to make sure they get what they need. That doesn't mean you should give up on meeting their needs.

I have met with parents who brought their son a chocolate milkshake in the morning because he got upset about having to get up to get ready for school. Do you think things got better? Of course not. If you are basing your decisions on making sure your child does not get upset, your child is in control of the family. That is too much responsibility for a child and ultimately it means that the child's needs are being neglected. In the chocolate milkshake example, it's obvious that what the child needs is to learn how to get up on time, get himself dressed and ready for school, and eat a nutritious breakfast. He needs to build coping skills and frustration tolerance. We all do. Trying to make sure he doesn't get upset is not what he needs, it's what his parents want. They were afraid to deal with an upset child. They were afraid that it meant they were bad parents and that their child wouldn't love them.

In Dr. Landreth's story he explains how upset his girls got about their choice. He also explains that if it was his choice, he would have chosen for them to get to watch TV. He didn't have to yell at his children or make them feel ashamed. He could empathize with them about how upset they were. The structure of choice-giving and giving his girls responsibility for their behavior provided what was needed. Dr. Landreth also explained that his girls "chose not to watch TV for 9 days." I remember being shocked when I heard that. If I had tried a consequence for a day or two and Dylan's behavior hadn't changed, then I would have believed it didn't work. The truth is, I didn't want to keep enforcing difficult consequences. If it's your child's choice, though, he gets to decide when he's ready to choose the more rewarding outcome.

My favorite thing about choice-giving is that it promotes good boundaries in your relationship with your child. Many problems that parents have with their children result from taking too much responsibility for things their children should be responsible for. For example, before I learned how to use choice-giving, mornings at our house were chaotic and stressful because I took responsibility for things my son should have taken responsibility for. I would wake up determined that this morning would be different, that I would drop Dylan off for school, both of us calm and happy, eager to start our day. The first problem was getting Dylan up in the morning. Determined to make things work out well, I attempted to wake Dylan up in a loving way, using my most encouraging and happy voice, reminding him that he needed to get up now so that he would have time to eat and get ready. Once he was sitting up, I asked him to promise me that he wouldn't fall back to sleep and ran to the kitchen to make breakfast and lunch. Things started to deteriorate, though, because Dylan didn't get up and get ready. It seemed that no matter how nice and encouraging I was, I could not get Dylan to get moving. Once he was up, things didn't get any better. Although he had laid his clothes out the night before, he had misplaced his sock while getting ready and he couldn't remember where he put his backpack. Although I had asked him several times to brush his teeth, he hadn't. When it was time to leave, we were both upset. He wasn't ready and I wanted to pull my hair out. After I learned choice-giving, though, I realized that the reason our mornings weren't working was that I was taking responsibility for things Dylan should be responsible for.

Before I implemented any choices, I sat down with Dylan and explained that I had been trying to show him that I loved him by doing things for him. I told him that I realized that if I kept doing things for him that he could do for himself that he wouldn't know how strong he was and he wouldn't learn how well he could do things on his own. I explained that I wasn't going to do things for him that he could do for himself because I loved him and I wanted him to know how strong he was and how well he could do things on his own.

My husband and I sat down with Dylan and explained our concerns about getting ready for school in the morning. We told Dylan how important it was to learn to get ready in the morning, because as a grown-up he would have to get up and get ready for work all by himself. Over a period of a few weeks we implemented choices to give Dylan responsibility for his behavior.

It's important not to give too many choices at once, because it will overwhelm your child. Begin with just one choice a week. For example, if your 8- to 18-year-old child is having trouble remembering to take his school supplies or keeping up with his backpack or homework, you can implement choice-giving by saying "If you choose not to have your things ready for school in the morning, you choose not to have those things at school. If you choose to have your things ready for school in the morning, you choose to have everything you need at school." When he comes home upset because he forgot his homework, you can be supportive and understanding, rather than shaming.

For a younger child, you may have a different more age-appropriate choice. The rule of thumb for choice-giving is

👍   Give big choices to big kids and little choices to little kids.[1]

A more appropriate choice for a young child related to keeping up with school stuff might be: "If you choose not to put your backpack where it belongs when you come home from school, you choose not to get to watch TV in the afternoon. If you choose to put your backpack where it goes when you get home, you choose to get to watch TV in the afternoon."

The most effective choice I ever gave my children was, "If you choose not to brush your teeth in the morning before it's time to go to school, you choose to eat raw vegetables for lunch, because that's the only thing that won't hurt your teeth. If you choose to brush your teeth in the morning before school, you choose to get to eat what you want for lunch." Giving this choice meant that all I had to do is check Dylan's toothbrush on the way out the door. I could stop asking him over and over.

I could stop nagging him and worrying about it. All I had to say about brushing his teeth was either "I see you've chosen to eat raw vegetables today" or "I see you've chosen to get to eat what you want to eat for lunch today." Regardless of what he chose, I could reflect his feelings about it by saying "You're really upset. Pizza was on the menu today and that's your favorite" or "You're really happy you didn't miss pizza today." That's the beauty of choice-giving; you give your child the responsibility for the behavior. Your responsibility is making sure to enforce the consequences in a loving, not a vengeful, way. Dylan chose raw vegetables only once. The rest of the time he chose to get to eat what he wanted for lunch.

One of the problems I had as a working mom in graduate school was coming home to the messes my children made. The problem was not just the mess but the time I had to spend with them being wasted on picking up their stuff and the tone of voice I used to ask my children to pick up their things. Using choice-giving I came up with a way to solve that problem. I gave my children their allowances in quarters rather than in dollar bills and implemented the choice "If you choose to leave something out of place, you choose to be charged a quarter for it. If you choose to put things where they belong, you choose to keep your money." This meant if I came home and saw a pair of socks and a pair of shoes on the floor in the living room, I said, "Oh Dylan, I see four quarters." My children responded by running into the room to pick up what I saw and pick up anything else I missed. They were usually smiling and laughing like it was a game to see who could find things to pick up before I did. They began helping each other, too. I'll never forget one evening I got home from work late. I was walking from the driveway up to the front door past the big picture windows in our living room. I could see my kids through the window running and jumping around trying to get everything picked up before I walked in the front door. They greeted me out of breath and laughing and the house was clean!

Can you imagine what that's like? The tone of the house had changed, especially in relation to getting it cleaned up. I didn't have to ask them to pick up, and if I found something out of place all I had to say was "I found a quarter" in a cheerful voice. The nagging and power struggles stopped.

The most important part of choice-giving is always following through with implementing the choices. If you don't, it won't work. If you've used threats in the past and didn't follow through, you know how ineffective your words become when you don't follow through. To make sure you follow through with a choice, you need to pick ones that work for you whenever possible so that you aren't punished every time your child chooses a consequence. I learned this the hard way one evening when I told Dylan, "If you choose to clean your room then you choose to get to go out to eat and to a movie. If you choose not to clean your room, you choose to stay home for the evening." Unfortunately, Dylan chose to stay home and since we didn't have a baby sitter, we did too. One of the better choices I gave was "If you choose to be disrespectful to someone, you choose to do one of their chores for them. If you choose to be respectful, you choose just to do your own chores." This meant that some days I got all of my chores done for me. Other days my children were respectful all day. Either way, you can't lose!

Teaching your child to be respectful is one of the most important responsibilities you have as a parent. Without respect for ourselves and others, our energy is drained—drained by trying to make ourselves into who we think we are supposed to be or drained trying to make others into who we think they are supposed to be. Respect can be defined as "holding someone in high esteem," "an attitude of acknowledging the feelings and interests of someone," or simply "to not interfere with." The last definition is, to me, the most important. Each one of us has a potential to become a loving, compassionate human being who has a lot to offer the world. As a parent I see it as my responsibility to stay out of the way of who my child is meant to be and teach him how to stay out of his *own* way so that he can be the person he was meant to be.

Sometimes, as parents, we believe that to gain our child's respect we must use fear—fear of punishment, fear of disapproval, and so on. There is a difference, though, between fear and respect. It's easiest to examine these differences by looking at the extremes. For example, imagine your reaction to being alone in a room and having to cooperate with the scariest person you can think of (for example, Hitler, Jeffrey Dahmer, or Darth Vader) and your reaction to the same situation with the most compassionate person you can think of (for example, Jesus, Buddha, Mother Teresa, or Obi Wan Kenobi). The most compassionate person you can think of most likely evokes respect associated with trust, openness, and acceptance, while the most fearful evokes either anger or a need to protect oneself. Even if you would treat people in both situations respectfully, it would not mean that you were treating them that way because you respected them.

These relationships also illustrate how respect is reciprocal in a relationship. The people you most respect are those who are the most respectful to you. It is difficult to imagine the most compassionate people in the example above trying to gain your cooperation by shaming or threatening you. It is difficult in situations in which we have no control to have faith in compassion rather than in fear, but given the above examples, it's clear that compassion is more powerful.

When we are stressed or feeling out of control, it is counterintuitive to try to see the world through someone else's eyes. In fact, when we are stressed and overwhelmed it seems the only way we can possibly survive the situation is for the other person to see the world the way we do and to comply with our wishes without any hesitation. To bend to the will of someone else regardless of your own feelings and interests, though, is not showing self-respect. To expect our child to give up his own self-respect to do what we think he should do without question is not respectful of our children's needs. It also undermines the trust we need in our relationship with children. How can our children trust or respect us if we don't care about their self-respect? Ultimately, respect for others can only come from self-respect.

👍   You can't give away what you don't have.[2]

If you asked me for a trillion dollars, I couldn't give it to you. Why? Because I don't have a trillion dollars. I can't give you what I don't have. To facilitate your child's respect for you, simply means to treat your child with respect, to be focused on your child's needs, and not interfere with who your child is meant to be.

Of course, no one is respectful all of the time. If you have made a mistake as a parent, apologize. Tell your children that you are sorry for yelling at them. Explain to them that they don't deserve to be yelled at or treated in a mean way. Explain also what the appropriate action would have been and what they can do if you or someone else yells at them or treats them disrespectfully. For example, if I yell at my daughter for being disrespectful to me, I can apologize by saying, "Deva, I was upset by what you said, but I shouldn't have yelled at you. I'm sorry, honey. I acted disrespectfully to you and that was wrong. I should have reminded you in a respectful way about our rule, that if you choose to be disrespectful, you choose to do an extra chore, so that is what I'm doing now. I also want you to know that when I yell at you or treat you disrespectfully, you may tell me, 'Mom, I'm not for yelling at.'"

It might be a little scary at first to empower your children this way, but imagine the impact, not just on your relationship but also on how your children will be able to stick up for themselves in a respectful way in any relationship. If you set up a structure in which you and your children are expected to act respectfully to each other, your children learn how to interact that way for the rest of their lives.

As parents learn to use compassion, ACT, and choice-giving, rather than shame or fear, they begin to realize there is no need for spanking. They also realize that hitting a child or anyone is disrespectful and that self-respect cannot be taught through spanking. Occasionally, parents have asked how they can be true to their faith without spanking. Many parents believe that "Spare the rod, spoil the child" is from the Bible. However, this verse is from a poem. The actual Bible verse is "He who spareth the rod, hateth his child." It's also important to note that the "rod" is traditionally used by sheep herders to keep away the wolves, not to beat the sheep with. Why would a sheep cooperate with a shepherd who beat him? Of course, we want to protect our children from the wolves. In Psalms the "rod" is referred to as something that comforts us (that is, "Thy rod and thy staff shall comfort me."). It makes sense to understand that the rod is used for protection and not for beating. Another consideration you might want to make if you are a Christian is, can you imagine Jesus spanking a child?

Many parents worry that nothing else will work as well as spanking at changing their children's behavior. Research, however, suggests that spanking can do more harm than good. For example, children who are spanked are more likely to have low self-esteem and to be involved in crime as adults. As discussed in this chapter, spanking does not promote self-control but rather requires an adult to exert control over the child.

It's understandable, though, why people are so worried about the consequences of not spanking. It seems that children, adolescents, and young adults are more disrespectful than ever. As a professor, I am utterly dismayed by the lack of respect for authority in our schools. It seems as though we are at a crisis point in our culture. I hear many people say that the reason there is such a problem is because parents and schools don't spank their children anymore. The research suggests, however, that an increase in corporal punishment in schools is correlated with an increase in behavior problems at school. I have also noticed that the students who are the most vocal about the necessity of spanking are the most disrespectful. As a therapist, I have noticed that families who spank a lot have higher levels of dysfunction and are more difficult to treat. However, in families that don't spank but don't set any limits at all, the problems are similar. It seems as though there is a large percentage of parents who think if they don't spank, they can't set limits. I have to admit, I was one of these parents. Because I associated all limit-setting with harsh, punitive measures, I didn't set limits when I should have. What I learned is that not setting any limits is as damaging as setting harsh ones. Either extreme is unhealthy. The beauty of using ACT and choice-giving the way it is described in this book is that you can use it whenever you need to without the worry of hurting your child or your relationship with your child. In fact, graduate students who were trained to use ACT set more limits than students in other training programs. In my experience in working with parents who spank, parents set more, not fewer, limits after using the methods I have taught them. That is because with spanking, you only use it when things get out of hand because it is so harsh. With ACT and choice-giving, you use it based on what boundaries the child needs to learn.

Choice-giving is even more effective when you use it as a household policy. Think back to the way Dr. Landreth introduced choice-giving: "I am instituting a new and significant policy within the confines of this automobile/household."[1] And the policy is, when you choose _____, you choose _____. If you choose _____, then you choose _____. As a policy, it doesn't need to be reestablished every day. It is a rule that applies across the board. So the next day if Dr. Landreth's girls fought in the car, he did not have to say, "If you choose to fight in the car, you choose not to get to watch TV, and if you choose not to fight in the car, you choose to get to watch TV." He only had to say, "I see you've chosen not to get to watch TV again today." Of course, his girls could say, "But Dad, you didn't tell us that today." To which he could respond, "Oh, you think that if I tell you a rule one day, it doesn't apply the next day? But girls, the choice I gave you yesterday was a policy and it will be true every day."

If they persisted, "That's not fair. We didn't know," he could say, "You're really disappointed. For some reason, you thought it was okay to fight in the car today. But the policy is the same today as it was yesterday. You can make a different choice tomorrow." Did you notice the last statement was just ACT? ACT and choice-giving fit beautifully together. In fact, before you use choice-giving, it is generally a good rule of thumb to use ACT two or three times. Once you establish a policy with choice-giving, though, you can use ACT to enforce it in a loving way. Below are some more example dialogues using ACT and choice-giving with the most common problems parents have with children. They represent the four most important target areas for families. I have seen many families transform by focusing their attention on changing the following four behaviors. I call them the Core Four. The Core Four are: treating others with respect, chores, getting in and out of bed, and homework.

Treating Others With Respect Scenario

Son: Moooom, Ashley hit me!

Daughter: Zach called me "Stupid Head!"

Mom: I know you're both upset. Zach, I know you were mad at your sister, but she isn't for calling names, and Ashley, I know you were mad at Zach for calling you a name, but he is not for hitting. If you are mad at each other, you can tell each other in a respectful way or you can hiss or growl at each other.

Son: She's too stupid to talk to!

Mom: Zach, I know you're upset, but Ashley isn't for calling names. You can draw a picture of you calling her a name or write a story about it.

Son: I wouldn't want to write a story about stupid Ashley.

Mom: I am instituting a new and significant policy within the confines of this household, and the policy is: If you choose to call each other names or treat each other disrespectfully, you choose to do an extra chore. If you choose to treat each other respectfully, you choose just to do your own chores. Which do you choose?

Daughter: He's the one who is stupid!

Mom: I see you've chosen to do one of Zach's chores.

Daughter: That's not fair! He called me stupid three times and nothing happened.

Mom: You think it's not fair, but once I instituted the policy it was your choice. If you want to talk about it some more, we can do that after you've finished doing a chore for Zach.

Daughter: That's not fair! (crying) I'm not going to do one of Zach's chores! You're always on his side!

Mom: I know it feels unfair. Zach didn't have a consequence and you did. But the moment you chose to call Zach a name after I instituted a policy, you were choosing to do one of his chores. After you do the chore, we can talk more if you want to.

Daughter: I'm not going to do it. (Screaming and crying)

Mom: I know you don't want to but you chose to. Let me know when you're finished and we can talk.

Note: There is no mention in this scenario of "tattletaling." I recommend not even introducing this term to children, because I have heard too many children say they didn't tell of abuse because they didn't want to be a tattletale. If your child is being overly controlling and critical of someone, instead of calling him or her a tattletale, use ACT. For example, say, "You're really worried about the way Susie is playing with the money. You think she isn't putting the money where it is supposed to go, but Susie gets to decide where the money goes when she plays with it. You get to decide when it's your turn to play." Or, "You really want to help me by telling your sister what to do, but I'm the mommy and I can do that. You can help by making sure you are following the rules."

Chore Scenario

> *Dad*: It's time to do your chores, Chris.
>
> *Son*: Daaaaad, I don't feel good. My stomach hurts.
>
> *Dad*: Let me check your forehead. You don't have a temperature. Even though you feel bad, it's time for doing chores. When you get through doing your chores, you may lie down.
>
> *Son*: That's not fair. I'm really sick and you don't even care! All you care about are chores.
>
> *Dad*: I know you think I don't care, but the rule is if you don't have a fever, you need to do your chores even when you feel bad. After you finish your chores, you may rest.
>
> *Son*: I'm not going to do them!
>
> *Dad*: I know you don't want to do your chores, but it's time for doing them. After you finish you can decide what to do.
>
> *Son*: I'm not listening to you.
>
> *Dad*: Chris, I am instituting a new and significant policy within the confines of this household and the policy is: If you choose not to do your chores, you choose to be grounded from everything, including TV, phone, computer, video games, and playing with friends. If you choose to do your chores, you choose to get to do what you want to do when you finish. Which do you choose?

Note: All children should have chores. It's important that they pick up their own messes and rooms and that they have at least one chore (for example, dishes, sorting or putting away laundry) that contributes to the family. It helps children feel valuable and competent to do their share. I don't, however, recommend paying children for chores. Children's allowances can be given to them just because they exist. If they don't contribute to the family in the ways you have asked, then they can be fined for that, rather than being paid for what they do.

The reason you don't want to associate paying your children an allowance with their contribution to the family is that they will expect to be paid for everything they do. It's really irritating to ask your child to do something and have her ask, "How much will you pay me?" or "Are you going to pay me for it?" I used to respond to my children when they asked this question by saying, "I will pay you for everything you do for me as long as you pay me for everything I do for you." After going over how much it would cost them, they decided to stop asking for payment.

In- and Out-of-Bed Scenarios

I've already explained how we got Dylan out of bed and ready for school using choice-giving. One important consideration if your child is having trouble getting up in the morning is whether or not he's getting to bed on time. The following shows how to use choice-giving to help your child to go to bed when she's supposed to.

Mom and Dad: It's time for bed.

Daughter: May I sleep in your bed, pleeeeeease?

Mom: I know you want to sleep with us, but bedtime is time for staying in your own bed. You may cuddle with us in the morning after 6 a.m. before we get up.

Daughter: But I'm scared (Crying). I don't want to sleep by myself.

Dad: I know you're scared, honey, but it's time for going to your bed. I will come and check on you and see how you are doing in a few minutes.

Daughter: Noooooo! I don't want to go to bed by myself. Please don't make me! (Screaming and crying).

Mom: I know you're scared, honey, but it's important to learn how to sleep in your own bed. You don't have to go to sleep right now, but it's time for staying in your bed. If you're scared, you can say prayers or cuddle Tiggey (her favorite stuffed animal). You can make up a story in your head about something you like or plan your next birthday party.

Daughter: (Calmer now, but stubborn) I am not going to sleep in my bed. I don't care what you say.

Dad: You don't have to sleep, but you have to stay in your bed. If you choose to get out of your bed, you are choosing to lose a privilege. If you choose to stay in bed, you are choosing to keep all of your privileges. Which do you choose?

Daughter: I don't care about my privileges. I'm going to your room to sleep. (Hops out of bed).

Mom: (Picking daughter up and putting her back in her own bed) I see you've chosen to give up TV in the morning.

Daughter: I don't care!

Dad: I know you don't care, you just care about sleeping with us, right now, but it's time for staying in your bed. I will be back to check on you in a few minutes.

Note: Bedtimes can be one of the most frustrating times for parents, especially if their child refuses to stay in bed. It's important to think of teaching your child to stay in bed in much the same way you handled your child when she was a baby. You had to get up several times during the night to check on her and deal with her distress. The same is true now. It's just one of the jobs you have to do as a parent. You didn't yell at your baby, you just did what you had to do. All kids should sleep in their own bed. It promotes coping skills and healthy boundaries. Bedtime routines are essential. Bath time, cuddle time, and story time are wonderful ways to end the day. Remember, though, that these times are off limits to consequences. No matter how difficult or misbehaved your children were, their bedtime routine should remain the same.

Homework Scenario

> *Mom*: Time to do your homework, Dylan.
>
> *Son*: Mom, Matt is supposed to come over to play!
>
> *Mom*: I know you want to play, but your homework has to be done first, then you may play.
>
> *Son*: But Matt is already coming over.
>
> *Mom*: You made plans, but you'll have to postpone them until your homework is done.
>
> *Son*: This homework is too hard. I'll never finish it.
>
> *Mom*: I know it feels impossible right now, but homework time is a time when you act the same way you would at school. Regardless of how you feel at school, you would try your hardest and you wouldn't argue with your teacher. After your homework is done we can talk about how difficult it was. In the meantime if you need my help, just let me know by asking in a polite way.
>
> *Son*: I can't do it!
>
> *Mom*: If you choose not to do your homework, you choose not to get to play with your friends. If you choose to do your homework, you choose to get to play with your friends. Which do you choose?

Note: You may also need to have a rule about grades. Generally speaking, if our children chose to get grades below Bs on their progress reports or report cards, they chose to be grounded. If they chose to make As and Bs, they chose to use their free time the way they wanted to.

Horse Sense

In his book *Horse Sense for People*,[3] the great horse whisperer Monty Roberts suggests posting the rules and consequences for children. I have found that this is a very good way for parents to be clear about choice-giving policies, and it also helps them follow through with the consequences when they are posted on the refrigerator. This method gives you another option in implementing choice-giving policy, also. For example, you can have a family meeting and implement the policy for chores on a poster before an argument ever comes up. You can implement a new policy each week, until you have the Core Four addressed.

Choice-Giving and Decision Making

Another way to implement choice-giving is by giving your child two choices in a difficult situation. For example, if your child doesn't want to take her medicine, you can say, "You may choose to take your medicine with grape juice or milk. Which do you choose?" If he is taking too long to decide what to wear, you can say, "You may choose to wear your blue shorts with the white top or your brown shorts with the green top. Which do you choose?" If your children want another option and you don't feel it's appropriate, all you have to say is, "I know you want to wear the sweater, but that's not a part of the choice. It's too hot outside. You may choose the white top or the brown one or I will choose for you."

Practice Choice-Giving

Use ACT and choice-giving to handle these situations:

1. *Your child refuses to get out of bed to get ready for school, explaining that she doesn't feel well. You've checked her temperature; it's normal, and she's not throwing up.*

2. *Your son is supposed to be doing homework, but when you check in to see how he's doing, he's playing video games.*

3. *Your child is never satisfied with the clothes she is wearing, complaining that they don't feel right, don't look right, or are uncomfortable. You've been considerate and chosen soft fabrics and made sure they fit properly, but no matter what you do, it's not good enough for your child.*

4. *Your child has a friend over to spend the night, but they won't be quiet and go to sleep.*

5. *Your child remembers to do his homework but can't find it when it's time to turn it in.*

6. *When your child plays video games, he becomes so frustrated and upset that he yells and hits things.*

7. *Your child misunderstood you and thought you said she could get a candy bar at the store. You're at the store and she's crying and screaming that you lied to her.*

8. *Your child has a new friend over and doesn't want to share any of her toys.*

Answers to Choice-Giving Practice

1. *Your child refuses to get out of bed to get ready for school, explaining that she doesn't feel well. You've checked her temperature; it's normal, and she's not throwing up.* Use ACT and choice-giving to handle the situation.

   ACT (three times): I know you're not feeling well or maybe you just don't want to go to school, but it's time to go to school, even if you don't feel like it. When you get home, if you still feel bad, you may rest.

   Choice-giving: If you choose not to get up, get ready for school, and get into the car on your own, on time, you're choosing to lose all of your privileges after school. If you choose to get up, get ready, and get into the car on your own without me having to put you in the car and make you go to school, you are choosing to get to do what you want to do after school. Which do you choose?

2. *Your son is supposed to be doing homework, but when you check in to see how he's doing, he's playing video games.* Use ACT and choice-giving to handle the situation.

   ACT (three times are not necessary or even recommended in this situation): I see you'd rather play video games than do homework, but it's time for doing homework. You may play after your homework is done.

   Choice-giving: If you choose to play video games before your homework is done and checked, you are choosing to lose the video games for the day (unplug the machine and lock it in your trunk if you need to). If you choose to get your homework done and have it checked, then you choose to get to play video games after your homework is checked. Which do you choose?

3. *Your child is never satisfied with the clothes she is wearing, complaining that they don't feel right, don't look right, or are uncomfortable. You've been considerate and chosen soft fabrics and made sure they fit properly, but no matter what you do, it's not good enough for your child.* Use ACT and choice-giving to handle the situation.

   Note: In this situation, have the child pick out the clothes she wants to wear for the next day the night before. If she won't pick something out, you can explain that if she chooses not to pick something out in the next 10 minutes, you will pick out something for her. The next morning if she still does not want to wear what she picked out, use ACT.

ACT: I know it doesn't feel the way you want it to, but you need to get dressed in either the blue shorts or the black pants right now, so we can get to school on time. When you get home, if it's still bothering you, you may put on your comfy dress.

Child: I don't want to wear either of those. They look stupid on me!

ACT: I know you don't like either of them, but it's time to pick one and put it on so we are not late for school. When we get home you may pick an outfit for the next day that you like.

Choice-giving: If you choose not to get ready on your own, you are choosing for me to dress you the best I can and to be grounded when you get home from school. If you choose to get ready on time by yourself, you are choosing to get to do what you want to do after school. Which do you choose?

4. *Your child has a friend over to spend the night, but they won't be quiet and go to sleep.* Use ACT and choice-giving to handle the situation.

ACT: I know you girls want to stay up and talk, but it's time to go to bed. You may talk and play tomorrow morning.

Choice-giving: If you choose to keep talking, you choose not to get to sleep in the same room. If you choose to be quiet, you choose to get to sleep in the same room. Which do you choose?

5. *Your child remembers to do his homework but can't find it when it's time to turn it in.* Use ACT and choice-giving to handle the situation.

ACT: It's so frustrating to do your homework and then not be able to turn it in. It's hard to stay organized. It takes practice. From now on, after you finish your homework, put it in your notebook where it belongs and bring it to me so that I can check your organization as well as your homework.

Choice-giving: If you choose not to put your homework in the correct place before you bring it to me to check, you choose not to get to watch TV for the day. If you choose to put it in the correct place before you bring it to me to check, you choose to get to watch TV for the day.

6. *When your child plays video games, he becomes so frustrated and upset that he yells and hits things.* Use ACT and choice-giving to handle the situation.

   ACT: I know it's frustrating when you lose, but this room is not for yelling and hitting in. If you want to yell, you can yell into your pillow and hit your pillow in your room with the door closed or you can come talk to me about how frustrated you are.

   Choice-giving: If you choose to yell and hit when you lose, you choose to put the game up for the day. If you choose to play calmly even though you're frustrated, you choose to get to play until your time is up.

7. *Your child misunderstood you and thought you said she could get a candy bar at the store. You're at the store and she's crying and screaming that you lied to her.* Use ACT and choice-giving to handle the situation.

   ACT: I know you're upset. You thought I said you could get a candy bar, but I did not say that or if I did it was a mistake. I understand how disappointed you are, but I'm not for yelling at and the store is not for making loud noises in. If you're upset you can talk to me about it when we get in the car. I can also hold you while you cry if you like. I know this is really disappointing.

> *Choice-giving*: If you choose to yell or make loud noises in the store, you are choosing to do an extra chore when we get home. If you choose not to yell or make loud noises, you are choosing to do what you want to do when we get home. Which do you choose?

8. *Your child has a new friend over and doesn't want to share any of her toys.* Use ACT and choice-giving to handle the situation.

> *ACT*: I know it's hard to share your toys, but when friends come over to play, it's time to share your toys. When they go home, you may have them all to yourself.
> *Choice-giving*: If you choose not to share your toy, you choose to lose the toy for the day. If you choose to share your toy, you choose to get to play with it for the day.

Review of Previous Homework

How did your feelings about yourself, your life, and your child change when you practiced fascination? Most parents experience being able to think more clearly and to "make room" for their child's feelings. How did keeping a "Doughnut Journal" have an impact on you? Continue to practice these exercises and notice how they transform you and your relationships.

Homework[2]

1. Practice giving one choice this week. (Don't forget to use the word *choose* four times and use a loving, not an angry, voice).
2. Have another play session practicing all of the skills you've learned (reflective listening, tracking, ACT, fascination); record the session and evaluate it.
3. Try to use the play session skills outside the play session when your buttons are pushed at least once this week.

7

Connecting With Your Child

Survival Tip 7

**You Are Everything
You See in Others**

As you begin to see the world through your children's eyes, you will become aware of the pain they experience. Old ways of dealing with that pain will be difficult to avoid. You may feel your rescue button pushed or you may detach yourself from your child. To be emotionally connected with our children requires us to be emotionally connected with ourselves. This becomes a problem because all of us try to escape our feelings at times. Our desire to deny or distract ourselves from our feelings is so strong that we can even use good things as a way to disconnect ourselves from emotions. For example, exercise or religion, two of the healthiest ways to cope with difficult emotions, can become as powerful and as insidious an addiction as any drug if used to escape our emotions rather than deal with them.

To work through emotions requires us to "sit" with them, to intently observe our reaction to them. Observing emotions without reacting to them allows them to guide us to a deeper, more meaningful connection with ourselves and others. Once you are able to observe emotions without reacting to them, you will be able to choose your behavior while experiencing an emotion. That is exactly what you are practicing in special playtime. You are closely observing your child, paying attention in a way that allows you to be emotionally attuned, and then, instead of reacting in a dysfunctional way as you have all of your life, you are reacting with the skills you have learned through reflective listening, tracking, and ACT limit-setting.

To use any of these skills, however, without allowing yourself to be empathic negates their effect. To truly be empathic is to feel in your heart the feelings of another person, or at least to try. If you use reflective responding without trying to experience the feeling, it will seem condescending or patronizing. When I first started to use a reflective response, my kids didn't like it because, without realizing it, I was using it as a technique to distance myself from the pain my children were experiencing. When you reflect, you stop taking responsibility for the feeling someone else is experiencing and just try to understand how they feel. However, if you understand the feeling logically and not emotionally, you distance yourself from the person. To experience and understand the feeling on an emotional level requires you to be adept at emotional coping, because if you experience the pain your child is experiencing it is difficult not to react by rescuing or fixing. I used to think that when I tried to fix or rescue my children from painful feelings I was reacting to my own needs and ignoring my children's needs, but what I came to realize is that when you meet someone's emotional needs in a relationship, you also meet your own. It was not my needs that I was responding to when I tried to rescue but rather what I wanted. I wanted their pain to go away, but what I needed was to learn how to be with them in the pain they were experiencing, and what my children needed was to learn how to cope with the pain we all experience in life.

My Own Chaos

By the third week of special playtime, Dylan was exclusively expressing chaotic themes during our sessions. He scattered all the toys and acted out an earthquake in the doll house. I felt as though I was unable to make a connection with him during these sessions, but I believe that, on an unconscious level, I had avoided making that connection. I know now that I was experiencing boredom because of my resistance to descend into Dylan's pain with him. I have found it to be true that, whenever I experience boredom during a play therapy session, it is due to my resistance to seeing the world through the child's eyes, because it reflects my own unresolved pain.

I had been experiencing a lot of grief over the changes that had taken place in my son, the loss of the relationship we once had, and feelings of helplessness I felt about not being able to take away the apparent pain he was experiencing. I became uncomfortable at the group meetings, afraid that my wounds and inadequacies would show. I felt distanced once again, this time with an intense awareness of the shame I carried. I soon found out, though, that my attempts to keep my feelings covered were useless in such an accepting environment. No matter how much I wanted to pretend that I felt happy and confident, my true feelings rose out of me as if they had been given a will of their own.

The unconditional love and acceptance that Dr. Landreth radiated and facilitated in the group were so powerful it was as if I had no choice but to allow all of myself to be present. As I shared my feelings, I felt both ashamed for letting them out and blessed that I had been able to. My feelings about parenting and my son became manifest, and so much of me that I had hidden or denied in the past was now a part of me again. The most wounded and vulnerable parts of me had been released, but so had the strength that contained them. My shame was transformed into grief by the acceptance offered in the group. Dr. Landreth and the group comforted me as I wept, but I had much more grieving to do than group time would allow. The caring words, gestures, and expressions that Dr. Landreth and the group gave to me during this session became a powerful image that I kept with me to give me the support I needed to face my most painful feelings. These images helped me to continue to grieve once I left the session.

As my feelings surfaced, I thought, at the time, that I was going over ground I had traveled before. I've heard so many clients and therapists express this same frustration, saying, "I thought I had already dealt with this." It seems to me now, though, that these familiar journeys are actually a deepening of experience. I will experience this pain and every feeling known to humankind over and over again, and each time I will have the opportunity to go deeper and deeper into that feeling. From this perspective, I am not continually reopening old wounds when I experience the pain that formed them; instead, I am passing through the doors they have made for me, traveling through their infinite pathways, each time finding a deeper level of understanding and a more meaningful connection with others.

Reconnecting

Due to the intense grief and lack of connection I was experiencing at the time, Dr. Landreth suggested that Dylan and I spend the time set aside for filial therapy doing something that would be fun and enjoyable for both of us. For the next two weeks the sessions were still nondirective and child centered, but we played outside, spontaneously deciding where to go or what to do next.

Once we had stepped out into the world, the possibilities seemed endless to both of us. During the second of these two sessions, Dylan and I rode our bikes to his school playground to play. What emerged was highly symbolic play directed by Dylan. He asked me to bury all but his head and his hands in a pile of sand. Once I had buried him, he said that I should pretend that I found him trapped there and I should come along and rescue him by holding his hands and pull him slowly out of the sand. This reminded me of how I had experienced the unconditional love and acceptance offered by Dr. Landreth. Our barriers to understanding seemed to melt away as I pulled him up to me and we embraced for a long time. I knew that a part of Dylan that had been hidden in darkness was now free. Next, he asked me to stand on one side of the field while he stood at the other so we could run to each other. When he reached me, we hugged and he asked me to whirl him around in my arms. Dylan had given himself and me an abiding memory of the connection we had made to each other and ourselves. On our way home from the playground, he requested that, for our next session, we use the special playtime toys in the room where we had previously had the sessions. He was ready to bring the endless possibilities of the world inside with us and so was I.

As I tucked him in that night he said, "Mom, I miss you."

He had said it so many times before, but this time I didn't feel guilty when he said it. I reflected, "You're wishing we could be together."

"Yeah," he said.

I wondered if his feelings were connected to jealousy over his younger sister Deva being with me while he was in school. I explored the situation. "Maybe you wish you could stay home with me during the day like Deva does," I queried.

"No," he said, "I like school and I need to go to it because I'm going to be a scientist. I just miss you."

"Oh," I said, "Missing me is one of the feelings you feel as you make your way in the world."

"Yeah," he said, "I want to decide what to do, but I miss you."

"I know, I miss you too," I said as I hugged him, "but I feel so proud as I watch you make your own way."

"It's tough out there, Mom," he said.

"Yes, it is," I reflected, "and I'm here if you need me." "I know," he said. Then he whispered and looked at me as he said "I love you, Mom."

"I love you too, Dylan." There we were, connected, but now also allowed to be separate. By encouraging Dylan to be who he was and not who I needed him to be or thought he should be, he and I began to know and enjoy who he truly was.

Following this session Dylan no longer complained about not being able to spend enough time with me, and his nightmares, fears, and obsession with aliens subsided. His drawings changed dramatically, becoming more organized and depicting peaceful scenes (Figure 7.1). He described this drawing as a walk down a country lane and seemed satisfied, contented, and peaceful as he drew and described his work. The white clouds could be symbolic of spiritualism. The eggs in the basket seem to be symbols of promising things to come, or anticipation of transformation. The path's perspective to the upward and right seems to indicate positive movement, while the tree on one side of the path is strong, straight and tall, indicating health and well-being. The trees on the other side of the path indicate strong needs, possibly for self-control or a return to the past to deal with past trauma. The tree that has fallen over the path seems to indicate an obstacle or past trauma that needs to be dealt with.

Figure 7.1

Themes of Struggle

The next few playtimes revealed themes of struggle. Dylan molded monsters out of the clay that would devour all the "good guys." He also liked to have battles with the army men and with me, asking if we could wrestle or shoot each other with the dart guns. For several sessions, his favorite thing to do was to tie me to a chair with masking tape. He would also tape odd things to me like diapers or toys, apparently wanting me to know what it was like for him to be humiliated.

At times I felt hurt by Dylan's desires to humiliate me, or guilty because he was experiencing such turmoil. Many times, I had to fight off the urge to rescue him, reminding myself that those feelings were related to my needs and not his. At other moments, though, I felt gratified by Dylan's play because I realized that he trusted me enough to let me know how he really felt.

Disclosure

The theme of the sessions changed again when Dylan asked if we could talk instead of play. During the first of these "talking" sessions, he revealed to me the depths of his loneliness and disappointment and spent most of the session crying in my arms. During the next two talking sessions, he told me things he had done that he was ashamed of. Both of these sessions ended with him being held like a baby in my arms at his request.

I was able to descend into Dylan's sorrow and shame only because I had developed a deep faith in his emotional experience. It was, of course, painful but also comforting to be with him in it, knowing that he would not have to deal with these feelings alone anymore. Through our sessions together I came to know that the chaos, pain, confusion, shame, and sorrow that Dylan experienced were feelings that deepened him, as they do all of us, and that trying to protect him from those feelings would limit him and our relationship. Facilitating the expression of Dylan's feelings taught me to trust in his ability to cope with life and heal his wounds.[1]

"I'm Worried About What My Child's Play Might Mean"

It is common for parents to become concerned about the play their children demonstrate during the play session. Sometimes it's difficult not to take personally whatever is being communicated in your child's play. It's important to remember that allowing them to play out whatever is there means that they don't have to deal with it alone. Trying to make them happy or see things the way you want them to see things will just keep them from showing you their pain; it won't make the pain go away.

If you are worrying about what your child's play means, you probably want to ask a lot of questions during the playtime. Remember that you don't have to know what your child's play means in order for your child to heal. It is the relationship that you are building with your child that allows healing to occur. By creating an accepting and loving environment in which your child is free to express feelings and thoughts, you are providing what is needed. If you are curious about what their play means, you can make statements that give them room to tell you about it. For example, if your child picks up the baby doll and makes it look as though it is running from something, you can track first by saying, "Looks like that baby is running." To explore the meaning you make room for your child to tell you by saying, "Maybe she's afraid or maybe she's just getting some exercise." You wouldn't ask, "Why is the baby running?"

If a child plays out a scenario with the toys that you know is related to something she or he is struggling with, then you can comment on it or wonder out loud about it. For example, if your child uses the dollhouse dolls to play out a fight you and your husband had that you didn't realize was overheard, you can say, "That Mom and Dad are mad at each other. Maybe you've heard Dad and me talk that way to each other." Refrain from asking, though, how that makes your child feel. If you have made room for your child to talk about his or her feelings, then your child will talk to you about it when he or she is ready.

If you are concerned that your child is revealing abuse to you through his or her play, it's extremely important to contact a professional as soon as possible who is trained in diagnosing and treating children who have suffered abuse. Any time you feel you are over your head, you should contact a professional, preferably one who is trained in filial therapy.

At times you may feel that your child's play is due to the mistakes you've made. You may even wish your child would reassure you that you are a good parent or tell you that you are forgiven for your mistakes. It's important to deal with these concerns outside the sessions with a professional or someone you trust. If you become aware of intense emotions during a play session, acknowledge them and then choose to use reflective responding, tracking, or ACT. Make a note to yourself to deal with these emotions later when your child is not around. This is, in effect, using ACT on yourself. For example, "I'm feeling guilty about how I've yelled and been mean to my child in the past and it's really difficult to see him acting it out with the toys. I can't deal with these feelings now because it's special playtime and I need to focus on my child's needs. I will call my best friend after I get through with special playtime or talk to my spouse after work."

Don't Let Your Excuses Get in Your Way

A father once said to me, "Being empathic just doesn't work for me." When I asked him to give me an example, he told me about an incident with his daughter. She had gotten hurt playing and didn't want to play anymore. He said he practiced empathy by saying, "I know you got hurt and you're scared to play now. I'll make sure you don't get hurt again, so let's go play." The father said that being empathic didn't work because the daughter still didn't want to play. I reflected, "So when you are being empathic, it is with the intention of getting someone to do what you want them to do." Immediately he recognized the problem. Being empathic to get someone to do what you want is not empathy, it is manipulation.

One way to relieve the stress created by seeing the world through your child's eyes is to find a reason to go back to old patterns of relating to your child. Thinking "This doesn't work with my child" is something you may tell yourself to get out of trying to practice healthier ways of relating to your child. If you're thinking like this (which is only human), you might not be getting what is being taught in this book, though. This book is not designed to help you make your child a different person. If you catch yourself thinking something like, "Making a loving connection doesn't work for my child" or "Healthy relationships don't work for my child," a truer statement might be "I am struggling to accept my child for who he is" or "I don't know how to have a healthy relationship with my child when he acts this way." All parents face this dilemma and have these feelings at times. We all have trouble accepting our children sometimes or understanding what they need from us.

"My Child Just Wants Attention"

When I was a child I heard, "He (or she) just wants attention" a lot, not about myself but about children who were in trouble or acting out. It made me feel guilty because I knew that I always wanted attention from my parents. Did that make me a bad kid? As I got older I continued to find this statement very confusing. I always want to say in response, "Well, give him some attention, then!" I can't imagine to this day what is wrong with wanting attention, particularly if you're a child. It's ironic that this statement shows why children behave in ways adults find irritating but at the same time discounts what the adult needs to do. The implied message is "This child is clearly showing through his behavior that he needs my help, but he obviously doesn't deserve it." A cartoon I was watching illustrated this point beautifully. Moms were at a swim class with their babies and the instructor told them, "If they sink to the bottom, don't help them, they're just trying to get attention."[2]

"My Child Is Trying to Manipulate Me"

The real issue is probably not that the child needs attention; it is probably that the adult feels manipulated by the child. If you find yourself feeling manipulated by your child or anyone else, ask yourself, "Why can't he ask for what he needs from me?" Being manipulative is asking for something you want or need in an indirect way. The cure is to ask directly. You can help your child learn how to ask for what he needs directly by using ACT. For example, "I know you really want my attention right now. You don't have to make up stories or talk in that whining voice to get my attention. You can just say, 'Mom, I need your attention.'"

"What About Discipline?"

When parents ask about discipline it usually means they are feeling out of control. You have been shifting your focus from shaping and molding your child to loving your child just the way he is. To focus so intently on how your child sees the world and being accepting of your child may leave you feeling out of balance if you haven't been using ACT a lot. It's difficult to stress how important ACT is. If you are feeling drained or taken advantage of, don't forget to say, "I know you need me right now, but I need some time to myself. You spend some quiet time in your room and we can talk more about this at 7:15." It's hard to let go of other disciplinary methods because they give you such a sense of power. To stop using shame and fear to control your children may leave you feeling powerless.

"I Don't Have Time for This"

I hear parents often say that their schedules are too busy or that they just don't have the time to do play sessions—but the play session is only 30 minutes, once a week. Surely, you can find 30 minutes once a week for the sake of your child's emotional well-being. If you truly do have too much to do to allow 30 minutes for your child's emotional needs, then there's something else you need to give up. I can't think of many things (if anything) that deserve priority over your child's emotional needs.

"No One Understands"

If confronting your excuses head on is making you feel that no one understands, it might mean you need more emotional support to get through the changes you are trying to make. Practicing these ways of being with your children is very difficult. In effect, it allows you to drop all of your psychological baggage, but sometimes it may feel that even though you've protected your child from it in the play session, it has come crashing down on top of you. Reach out to a friend, pastor, or professional who can help support you. Look for someone who will not try to fix or rescue you, but rather, someone who will be with you in whatever you are experiencing.

"I'm Worried I'm Not Doing It Right"

Without a group or a trained filial therapist, you might start to worry whether you are doing the play sessions the way you are supposed to. It might be a good idea to talk to a filial therapist in your area if you feel you're just not getting it. You can also visit www.specialplaytime.com to find resources available to you.

A really effective way to supervise yourself is to transcribe a videotape of a play session with your child, jotting down the feelings you have whenever you or your child responds. Below is an example of how to do the exercise.

Child: (Playing with the dollhouse dolls, pretending all of them are kids at school. One that he has identified as himself is being picked on by the other dolls.) Get out of here. We don't want to play with you!

Parent feeling: Heart aching, hurt for him, wishing I could take the pain away.

Parent: Those are bad boys, but you're good. They're jealous of you because they know you're better than them.

Child: (Stops playing with the dolls and says he's bored)

Parent feeling: Realizes that trying to make my child feel better gave him the message that he shouldn't talk about this situation with me, that I couldn't handle the pain he was feeling: Feeling guilty, wanting to make things better.

Parent: Oh you can play with those toys. Go ahead, tell me again how they were mean to you. I'll just listen.

Child: (Withdraws further) I want to leave now. Can we stop? I'm hungry.

Parent feeling: Guilty, frustrated, hopeless.

Parent: Oh come on. Let's play, we'll have fun. Come on. I'll do whatever you want to do.

Parent feeling: Desperate.

Child: (Whining and pretending to cry) I'm hungryyyyyyy! I want something to eeeeeat! (Lays down on the floor crying).

Parent feeling: Frustrated, hopeless.

Parent: Okay, fine. Let's go get something to eat.

Analyzing the Transcript

Clearly, this parent has let her feelings take control of the session. She is reacting to her wish to rescue her child and escape her guilt rather than focusing on what her child needs. We all do this sometimes, myself included. Below is the transcript with notes on analysis and corrections added.

Child: (Playing with the dollhouse dolls, pretending all of them are kids at school. One that he has identified as himself is being picked on by the other dolls.) Get out of here. We don't want to play with you!

   Parent feeling: Heart aching, hurt for him, wishing she could take the pain away.

Parent: Those are bad boys, but you're good. They're jealous of you because they know you're better than them.

   Analysis: Parent is leading the session, trying to make her son feel the way she wants him to feel rather than being with him in the feeling.

   Do's and don'ts to follow: Do let the child lead; Do reflect feelings; Don't give information or teach; Don't preach.

   Skill to use: Reflective response: "Looks like he's having a rough day."

Child: (Stops playing with the dolls and says he's bored)

   Parent feeling: Realizes that trying to make my child feel better gave him the message that he shouldn't talk about this situation with me, that I couldn't handle the pain he was feeling. Feeling guilty, wanting to make things better.

Parent: Oh you can play with those toys. Go ahead, tell me again how they were mean to you. I'll just listen.

   Analysis: Parent is leading the session, trying to make her son feel the way she wants him to feel, rather than being with him in the feeling.

   Do's and don'ts to follow: Do let the child lead; Do reflect feelings.

   Skill to use: Reflective responding "You didn't like what I said about the bullies being jealous of you. It made you feel like I don't understand what it's like at school."

Child: (Withdraws further) I want to leave now. Can we stop? I'm hungry.

Parent feeling: Guilty and a little desperate.

Parent: Oh come on. Let's play, we'll have fun. Come on. I'll do whatever you want to do.

Analysis: Parent is leading the session by fixing, trying to make her son feel the way she wants him to feel, rather than being with him in the feeling.

Do's and Don'ts to Follow: Do let the child lead; Do reflect feelings; Do set firm and consistent limits.

Skill to Use: ACT—"I know you're hungry, but it's not time for eating right now. You can have a snack when we're through."

Child: (Whining and pretending to cry) I'm hungryyyyyyy! I want something to eeeeeat! (Lays down on the floor crying).

Parent feeling: Frustrated, hopeless.

Parent: "Okay, fine. Let's go get something to eat."

Analysis: Parent is leading the session by rescuing, trying to make her son feel the way she wants him to feel, rather than being with him in the feeling.

Do's and Don'ts to Follow: Do let the child lead; Do reflect feelings; Do set firm and consistent limits.

Skill to use: ACT—"You're really upset. You want something to eat now, but it's not time for eating right now. We have 15 minutes left in our playtime. You can have a snack when we're through."

This exercise provides many insights. As you can see, if you stick to the "Do's and Don'ts" and use only the basic skills of reflective responding, tracking, and ACT, you will be on the right track. This exercise also shows how reacting to your feelings rather than understanding them can change your focus from trying to understand what your child needs to trying to make yourself feel better. Even though most of us in this situation would believe that we were being guided by what our child needs, it's clear when you look closely that is not the case.

"How Is Understanding My Feelings
Different From Reacting to Them?"

In the above scenario, had the parent understood the feeling of guilt she was experiencing rather than reacted to it, she would have known that the guilt indicated that she had gotten off track and was no longer focusing on her child's needs. When the guilt took control of the session, it was because she was desperate to get rid of the feeling and make everything the way it was "supposed" to be. Connecting with our feelings in a meaningful way means that we learn to trust them rather than try to get rid of them.

As discussed in chapter 4, our emotions relate to our desire for personal power. The emotions we struggle with are those that make us feel powerless. Anger always starts with a feeling of powerlessness. It is an attempt to gain control where we feel powerless. Sadness is giving up hope. Hope is a belief that things can work out the way we want them to. Grieving is letting go of sadness. In other words, grieving is letting go of the hope that things will work out the way we want them to. Depression is holding on to sadness, dwelling on the fact that things are not going to work out the way we want them to. At the heart of our resistance to our emotions is the fear of grief, the fear of letting go of the way we wish things could be. This process of letting go of hope, of our desire for power, is to grieve. To let go of our desire for personal power is to be happy. Grieving allows us to let go of how we want things to be so that we can accept things as they are. It is our ability to accept ourselves and our situation that allows us to find happiness.

Are You Still Grieving Your
Own Childhood?

The way you cope with emotions and relate to others' emotional needs is largely a result of how your parents related to your emotions when you were a child. As you've learned in this book, parents with the best of intentions can sometimes neglect their children's emotional needs.

It's important to explore how your emotional needs were addressed as a child. What did your mother do when you scraped a knee or fell down? What did your father do? What did your mother do when you were sad? What did your father do? What was comforting to you as a child? Who comforted you? Who or what made you anxious? Who did you talk to about the things or people who made you anxious? What hurt you most as a child? How did your parents react?

Answers to these questions that might indicate your emotional needs were neglected include those in which your pain was ignored or you were asked to pretend you weren't hurting. Some people may even remember instances when their pain made their parents mad, such as when parents say, "If you don't stop crying, I'm going to give you something to cry about." This statement is a clear indication of neglected emotional needs.

Another important question to ask yourself is "What is your biggest fear for your child?" or "What are you most afraid of as a parent?" The answers to these questions may reveal a lot about what guides your decisions and behavior. It's also important to ask yourself how the fears you have relate to the problems you are having with your child. Finally, ask yourself what you could forgive and what you want to feel forgiven for. Specifically, what do you wish you could forgive your parents for and what do you wish they would forgive you for?

Connecting with the most difficult times of your childhood brings up painful emotions that most likely have not been worked through. They may be as raw and excruciating as they were the day they were created. Emotions that aren't processed have a way of making their way back into our lives until we figure out how to deal with them.

I saw a man who had suffered so much shame and emotional abuse as a child that he had worked his entire life trying to get rid of it, but, of course, it didn't work. None of us have the power to get rid of a part of ourselves. We have all been born whole and will always be whole, whether we are aware of it or not. In therapy as he tried to reconnect with the shame his father had put on him, I became aware that one of the things that got in the way of his healing was the pain he felt for unintentionally shaming his children in the same way. I asked him to tell a story about the last time his father had shamed him. He told a story about when he was a young adult and had spent a few pennies on a sticker for his car. His father criticized him for it, telling him that he shouldn't waste his money on such foolish things. In itself, this was not a big deal, but it was linked in my client's mind to the criticism he had suffered all his life and the harsh beatings he had endured. The reason this story stood out in my client's mind is because it was the first time he could remember sticking up for himself when his dad criticized him. After empathizing with my client about how he must have felt, I asked him to imagine empathizing with his father. What feeling was driving your father all of those years? What drove him to shame you, humiliate you, and scare you? At first he was very resistant, even angry that I had asked him to empathize with his father. For weeks he simply refused to do it. He believed that I was trying to show him how ashamed he should be of himself. Eventually, after he had learned to trust me, he struggled to figure out what drove his father. I asked him to imagine himself in the position of criticizing one of his children for spending too much money and reminded him that all parents criticize their children sometimes. He immediately realized that his father was worried. He looked up at me and asked, "Worried? My father was worried about me? That's what all of that was about? My God, why didn't he just tell me he was worried about me? That would have been so different." In fact, most of the mistakes we make as parents we make out of worry: worry about how our kids will turn out, worry about their ability to find happiness, worry about the harm we've caused.

Identifying Your Own Emotional Issues

One way to find out what emotional issues might be getting in the way of your relationships is to do the following exercise. Take a pen and paper and write out the following sentence: "I don't like _____ because he/she is _____." Now, don't think you can get away with saying, "I like everybody." That is called denial. If you can't think of anyone you know, though, you can use a famous person or a politician. You can also think of a particular characteristic of a person you don't like. "I don't like _____ when he/she is _____."

Now write the following sentence: "I don't like myself because I am _____, and put in the blank whatever you put in the last blank for the person you don't like. Ouch! Everybody hates this exercise.

The only time this might not work is when we are too specific or too general. For example if you say, "I hate my boss because she is a drug addict" and you are not a drug addict, ask yourself to get more specific. What is it about her being an addict that you hate? Is it that she's irrational? Hurtful? Doesn't take responsibility? Those things are true of all of us at some time or another. The truth is, we are all we see in other people, myself included. I am nice, but the opposite is also true. (Just ask the lady at Sally Beauty Supply who wouldn't take back my blow dryer that stopped working after a week because, although I had my receipt, I didn't have the box it came in.) I am smart, but the opposite is also true. (You may be thinking, "Yeah, you're dumb if you think I'm the thing I hate about that other person.")

Now here's the good news. The opposite is also true. Take out a pen and piece of paper again. This time though, think of a person you really admire. It can be someone you know or someone famous. Now list three qualities you admire about this person. As you look over the qualities, remember, these are qualities that describe you too.

Review of Previous Homework

I wish I could hear about your choice-giving practice! Parents are always amazed at how well this skill works. Hopefully, you have started being able to use the skills you have learned in the most frustrating situations. That is a sign you have mastered the skills. However, no one can use these skills all the time. Just remember, if you forget to use a skill when you should have, go back and apologize to your child and tell him or her what you should have said (for example, "I shouldn't have yelled at you. I should have said, I understand how tired you are, but this half of the house is not for talking that way in whining voice. If you're tired you can go rest for a while and then come back and talk to me in your normal voice.")

Homework[3]

1. Practice the "I am everything I see in others" exercise whenever you are irritated by someone or feel like judging him or her.
2. Have a play session; record and evaluate it.
3. Use the play session skills as often as you can remember outside the play session, especially when your buttons are pushed.

8

NURTURING YOUR CHILD'S INNER WISDOM

> **Survival Tip 8**
>
> It's Difficult to Enjoy
> Your Child If He or She
> Is a Measure of Your
> Success as a Parent

We are all born with an innate wisdom and a capacity to love, to heal, to give to others, and to make our lives meaningful. This humanistic concept has been confused as being a secular idea that denies the existence of God. However, humanism is deeply spiritual. It teaches compassion and reliance on and faith in a power beyond us, a wisdom more powerful than we are. All of the major religions refer to this wisdom as something we must accept within ourselves. Christianity refers to the Christ spirit within, Buddhism refers to Buddha Nature, and Hinduism refers to Brahman.

There is a tendency to believe that this wisdom must be "put into" our children by us, but it is beyond anything one person could do for or to another person. In healthy relationships we learn to rely on this inner wisdom rather than be controlled by someone else. We are guided in a healthy relationship to find the answers within ourselves, to trust our conscience and our gut feelings. We strive to be who we were meant to be rather than who we are supposed to be. To practice this as parents is to allow yourself and your child to be guided by something more meaningful than any human idea of what people should be.

Three Conditions for a
Healthy Relationship

Carl Rogers, the founder of person-centered theory, the theory on which "child-centered" play therapy is based, brilliantly outlined three conditions for a healthy relationship. They are simply translated as: "I love you, no matter what; I'll see the world through your eyes; and I'll be honest." While most people think they practice these conditions, especially as parents, most don't. In fact, it's impossible to practice these conditions all of the time. The special playtimes you have been having with your child are specifically designed so that you can practice child-centered play therapy and these three conditions associated with the model for 30 minutes each week. Thirty minutes a week might not seem like much time to have a healthy relationship, but it's more than most people ever experience. The conditions for a healthy relationship are so powerful, that practicing them just 30 minutes once a week can have a profound impact.

Making Love Conditional

As discussed in chapter 1, as parents we get off track from these conditions by having our own agenda. We want our children to be smart, beautiful, hardworking, cooperative, and reliable. We think of ourselves as shaping and molding our children into "good" human beings. We constantly evaluate whether or not they are becoming the persons we think they should be. We evaluate ourselves the same way. If our child makes a bad grade or acts inappropriately, we think that means we are "bad" parents. We feel the weight of responsibility and our failure to make our children into the people we were supposed to make them into. We panic and try to see where we've been "too soft" or "too loving" and vow to not let our children ever get away with anything again for fear if we do we may ruin them forever. This constant evaluation of yourself and your child interferes with your relationship. It's difficult to enjoy your child if he or she is a measure of your success as a parent.

Praise, the Language of Evaluation

A lot of evaluation is unconscious. For example, when you use praise, you are evaluating your child and trying to shape and mold him or her into the person you think he or she should be, either someone with a particular talent or one who has high self-esteem. Praise is a language of evaluation. It communicates the opposite of "I love you no matter what." Instead, it communicates, "I love you when you're good." It is also used a lot of times in a manipulative way. For example, saying "You're so wonderful for taking your dish to the sink! I'm so proud of you for doing that!" is an attempt to control your child's behavior in a way that isn't supposed to feel controlling. Another way we use it in a controlling way is by trying to make our children feel good about themselves. For example, saying "You are the smartest person in the class" may be an attempt to increase self-esteem. However, rather than increasing self-esteem, it likely increases the pressure a child feels to live up to parental expectations.

A Misunderstanding of Self-Esteem

There has been much emphasis put on praising children, and it's really frustrating to realize that praising can be a problem. You've probably worked hard to praise your children as much as you could because you believed it was good for their self-esteem. Self-esteem is misunderstood in our culture, however. Having self-esteem does not mean feeling as though you are "good" or the best. It doesn't mean that you like everything about yourself, either. Self-esteem is more akin to self-acceptance. It means you are accepting of all of yourself, flaws and gifts alike. It means you don't feel the need to be perfect because you're comfortable with the way you are.

Praising to enforce good behavior and high self-esteem also teaches children to be guided by what other people think, rather than their own inner wisdom. It teaches them to be dependent on others for a feeling of self-worth. For example, if your child draws a scribble and you say, "Oh that's beautiful," your child is likely to go back and draw another scribble that looks like the one that was praised. Instead of being guided by his or her own creativity, he or she is being guided by what you think. If you have said something is pretty or good when it's not, just to make your child feel good, your child is being guided by something that isn't even true.

Sandy Blackard, author of *Say What You See for Parents and Teachers*,[1] a booklet based on filial therapy, explains that praising can lead to mistrust, even when the parents believe what they are saying:

> Children accept praise only if they already agree. If children have a different opinion of themselves, praise can break trust. For example, if we praise children for being smart or pretty and they don't already believe they are, they may either think we're just being nice and won't be able to trust us to tell them the truth, or they will think we don't understand them. In both cases, their belief that to be accepted they have to be something they are not will be confirmed. For building self-confidence and connecting with children, acknowledgment is the best choice.

Helping children build self-confidence allows them to find their "inner voice," their own wisdom. To be guided by your own wisdom or "inner voice" requires practice just like any other skill. When you consistently guide your children toward their own internal valuing process, they learn to rely on it rather than the external reward of someone else's approval. We all know that work we do for personal satisfaction is much more rewarding than work we do for a paycheck. We are more likely to be productive when guided by the enjoyment of doing something rather than an external reward. Research studies support this idea. Children who were rewarded for reading chose not to read when the reward was not available. Children who read for the internal satisfaction inherent in reading tended to read often. To help your children focus on their own internal valuing process is to teach them to lead productive lives aligned with their values and what makes their life meaningful rather than status seeking or striving to gain other people's approval.

Ideal Self versus Real Self

If your child is guided by your evaluation, he or she creates an "ideal self" that he or she is always striving to become. Striving for the ideal self guides us away from our "real self." Our ideal self is who we think we are supposed to be, rather than who we really are. Rather than being guided by our own inner wisdom or who we really are, we try to be who we think we should be, who we think others want us to be. We may also become perfectionists. A perfectionist never feels "good enough," because regardless of how hard he or she tries, there is always room for improvement. If your feelings of self-worth are based on how well you have done, then you begin to believe that what makes you lovable is that you are really good at something. You can also start to believe that whoever is the best at something is the most lovable. Not being the best translates into not being loveable. Eventually, the impossible quest of trying to be perfect or be the best at everything leads to burnout. When this happens, typically during a major transition such as beginning junior high, high school, or college, you see a dramatic and abrupt shift in behavior or appearance. For example, the straight-A student starts failing classes or the "girl next door" starts dressing in black and wearing her hair in her face. The "perfect" child becomes the "bad" kid.

I Love You, No Matter What

To avoid the problems created by praising and evaluating your child, you can simply "prize" or value your child for just existing on the planet. In reality, there is nothing your child can do to make you stop loving him or her. If you tell your child that, and then evaluate him or her, you may be sending your child a mixed message. To consistently communicate to the child that "I love you no matter what" focuses on what the child does specifically to create a desired outcome. It's just what you've been doing in special playtime when you "say what you see."[1] If your child takes his dish to the sink, say, "I noticed you took your dish to the sink. You're helping keep the kitchen clean." If you child makes straight As and is beaming with pride as she shows you her report card, say, "You are so proud of yourself. You worked really hard and it paid off." If your child brings you a scribble and says "Mommy, look what I did," don't worry, you don't have to evaluate it, simply say, "Oh look, you started right here and went up and down and all around and then ended right here and you did it all by yourself!" Instead of saying "I'm so proud of you" or "Good job," which focuses on what you think or feel, you focus on what the child does or feels, saying "You're so proud of yourself," "You did it," or "You're getting that just the way you want it." These responses can be referred to as "centering responses." The following quotes from *Say What You See*[1] explain why these types of responses are so valuable.

For children to see their strong points, we must see them first. Centering responses point out children's strengths. They are responses that strengthen a child's sense of self and build self-confidence. Centering responses are all about the child. [These responses use acknowledgment to help the child develop inner strength.]

To help children become centered and look inward, use objective acknowledgment rather than praise whenever possible. Children act according to who they believe they are, just as we do. If I believe I am a parent or teacher, I will work to become a good role model for children; if I believe I am an artist, I will draw; if children believe they are smart, they will pursue a college degree; if children believe they are considerate, they will become aware of others' feelings.

Acknowledgment affirms who the child is. Our beliefs about who we are most often come from our successes and failures—those of which we are aware. By watching for and acknowledging children's successes, we can make them aware of their inner strengths so they can define themselves accordingly. Acknowledgment has far greater impact on a child's idea of self than praise. Praise is about what we think and what we like; acknowledgment is about the child. Acknowledgment builds confidence because it says who the child is, not just what we think.[1]

Using acknowledgment, you can further highlight your child's strengths by adding a positive conclusion about the child's actions. The importance of this is explained in *Say What You See*.

To acknowledge a child objectively, Say What You See, and add a *strength*. By adding a strength after you Say What You See, you are tying your comments to immediate, objective observations and providing children with proof instead of opinions. Saying, for example, "You read the book and figured out how to solve the math problem yourself. That shows you are smart" makes the child's intelligence undeniable.

All children have every inner strength; they just don't know it. When you want a child to see a particular strength, watch for it in everything the child does. Start with the basic building block, Say What You See, and name the strength to prove to a child it's there. For example, "You finished making that, even though you seemed frustrated at times. That shows you are determined," or "You told me right away that you spilled the milk. That shows you are responsible."

Sometimes you might not realize you saw an example of a strength until later. No matter; kids allow do-overs. You can go back at any time, point out what you saw, and name the strength then. Children love it when they hear that they've gotten your attention even when they were not with you. Similarly, if you hear yourself use praise, follow it immediately with an acknowledgment of what you saw and add the strength it represented. The evidence presented in the acknowledgement will validate the praise.

Additional centering comments to use when you Say What You See include: "You did that just the way you wanted to!" or "It's what you think that matters!" or and "You stopped yourself!" Picture children growing up with powerful thoughts like these to guide them. Teens and preteens who believe their opinions matter and believe they have self-control look inward rather than to peers for approval.[1]

Valuing Not Evaluating

The prizing or valuing of your child is communicated in the tone of your voice and the intention in your heart, not to shape or mold your child but to love him or her. The tone of your voice communicates what you feel in your heart that your child is lovable just the way he or she is. There is nothing your child can do, "good" or "bad," to change how much you love him or her. It is the feeling you had when your child was a baby. Your child didn't have to achieve anything or be "good" for you to value him or her. You valued your child just because he or she was born, just because he or she existed on the planet.

You're Already Doing It

To communicate to your children that you love them even when they make a mistake requires a shift from punitive, shaming methods to loving firmness and structure. If you have been practicing ACT and choice-giving, you have made the shift. By communicating to your children that you can act in a loving way even when they make a mistake, you are creating a relationship in which your children can turn to you when they make a mistake or even better, when they are afraid they will make a mistake. The reason we didn't tell our parents about our mistakes, or discuss with them the mistakes we were afraid we would make without their guidance, was because we feared the shame, disappointment, and rejection we would face.

By practicing reflective responding (for example, "You are angry because I asked you to clean up your room"), you have also been practicing the language of "I love you no matter what." When you use reflective responding, you are communicating that you can accept your child just as he or she feels. You put your own desires aside for him or her to be happy all of the time or see things the way you do to be with you child in a loving supportive way just as he or she is at that moment.

I'll See the World Through Your Eyes

Whenever you make a reflective response, you are also practicing the second condition of a healthy relationship, to see the world through your child's eyes or empathize with your child. Most power struggles and arguments we have are a result of not providing this condition in a relationship. If we could translate all power struggles into the simplest of terms they would all sound the same: "I'm right and if you don't see it the way I do, then you're wrong." "No, I'm right and if you don't see it the way I do you're wrong." "I'm right because of this, this, and this. That means you're wrong." "No, I'm right because of this, this, and this. That means you're wrong." It goes on and on like this with each person trying to make the other one see things through his or her eyes. When couples say that they've had the same argument for years and it never gets resolved, this is what they are talking about. Neither person is willing to provide empathy to the other one because being right becomes more important than understanding.

The same thing happens in our relationships with our children. We start to believe that we have to get them to see things the way we do. For example, if your child says, "I hate school!" you may be tempted to get her to like school or appreciate it by saying, "Oh school is important. It's something you should like." Instead, all you need to say is "School is really frustrating." If your child says, "You're mean for making me clean my room," you may be tempted to say, "I'm not mean because I want you to do chores." Instead all you need to say is "Hmm, you think I'm mean if you have to pick up your mess." If your child says, "I hate my sister," you may be tempted to say, "No you don't, you love your sister because she's your family." Instead, all you need to say is, "You're angry at your sister." By arguing in these situations, we create unnecessary power struggles. It is not essential that our children see things the way we do. In fact, even if a limit is needed, it is their perspective that matters. We have to give up being "right" and just understand where our children are coming from. Without that understanding, it is impossible to guide them.

I'll Be Honest

Essentially, the three conditions for a healthy relationship are a formula for compassion. To practice compassion is to practice faith in love, rather than faith in hate. Most of us believe that we have more faith in love than hate, but when we become frustrated we are much more likely to turn to violence or punishment than we are to compassion. We become defensive and controlling, trying to get the other person to behave the way we want. When we have more faith in hate, we feel the urge to spank, shame, or punish. We want to get revenge or teach our child a lesson. We stop having faith in our child and in compassion, thinking that we have to "make" our child behave appropriately. We tell ourselves that acting with compassion means being weak. This belief is usually a misunderstanding of compassion that leaves out the condition to be honest.

Honesty in a relationship is what allows us to have good boundaries. If you practice the first two conditions of a healthy relationship without a commitment to being honest, you will likely feel taken advantage of. If your needs are neglected in a relationship, the relationship is not a healthy one. Many times we confuse what we want with what we need and impose our wishes or desires at the expense of the other person's needs, or vice versa. Being honest with yourself will help you understand what your needs are and what your child's needs are. It will also help you to understand that meeting either person's needs in the relationship will meet both people's needs. While it is not appropriate to ask your child to meet your needs, getting your needs met is essential to having a good relationship with your child.

Sometimes we forfeit honesty because we're afraid to hurt someone's feelings or we're afraid they'll be upset. If you are walking on eggshells or trying not to upset someone, though, you're not being honest either about your feelings or what your needs or the other person's needs are. For example, I used to have a client, a little boy, who came to see me because he was having difficulty getting along with others and cooperating with his teachers and parents. He had suffered a great deal of emotional abuse, having to lie for his mother who had been cheating on his father. His mother lied to him about many things. He had learned to trust no one. He feared if he told the truth or even confronted his mother about her lies, he would be abandoned by her. He was just 11 years old when his mother finally did abandon him.

During our session one day, he began to tell me a story about a two-headed dog that I just couldn't believe. Typically I would have gone along with the story as if I were participating in a fantasy with him, to understand him on a deeper level, but then he posed a challenge to me by saying, "You believe me, don't you? You know I'm telling you the truth, right?" At that moment, I realized that he was working on the issues he had about lying in his relationship with his mother. I knew if I honestly told him that I didn't believe him, he would be upset. I worried about hurting him and damaging our relationship. He had been accused of lying a lot and made to feel guilty both for telling the truth and for not telling the truth. I knew that if I didn't tell him the truth I would be rescuing him and making the relationship unhealthy. I practiced honesty by telling him, "I wish I could believe what you were telling me, but I don't know how to make myself. I can pretend that it's true, if you would like me to." He immediately became very upset and angry, yelling, "You're just like everyone else. You don't believe anything I say. I hate you and I don't ever want to come back. What kind of therapist doesn't believe a child!" I understood that he was saying almost exactly what had been said to him by his mother: "What kind of child doesn't believe his mother!" I reflected, saying, "I know it hurts your feelings. It feels to you like I don't care about you if I say I don't believe you, but it's not that. I just don't know how." He then said, "How can you care about someone who lies?" I realized that he had been trying to understand how to love his mother, while acknowledging her lies and how she had hurt him. I explained that everyone makes mistakes and that the mistakes people make don't make me stop caring about them. He then climbed up in a special chair in the playroom and announced, "Okay, from now on, this is the truth chair and whenever I sit here, I tell the truth." I was worried I was in for a struggle, but he surprised me by admitting that the story wasn't true. I empathized with him, imagining how difficult it must be to tell the truth after making up a story, and I said that I might make up such a story because I wanted to be interesting to the other person. He opened up further, explaining that he made up stories a lot to try to get people's attention. He also started to explain how his mother had hurt him and how he believed he had hurt his mother.

Regardless of how much I practice honesty, it's still difficult for me when I know my honesty will upset someone. To be honest in that situation requires me to put my own wishes aside to keep the peace, to keep others happy. I used to think it was my need to keep others happy, rather than my wish, but I realized that what I needed most was to be honest. This is an example of how, when you meet one person's emotional needs in a relationship, you usually meet both people's needs.

There is so much confusion about what a child needs, as opposed to what a child wants, that it spurred a movement in the mental health field to move from a "child-centered" approach to a "family-centered" approach. Some authors incorrectly stated that a child-centered approach disrupts the family by asking parents to relinquish their authority.[2] They describe parents who use a child-centered approach as those who were "asking children whether they want to go to school or trying to convince a toddler to agree that it's dangerous to play in the street." This misunderstanding of a child-centered approach is due to the belief that you need only implement the first two conditions of a healthy relationship.

If your child is demanding, it may be because you have focused too much on the first two conditions and not enough on the third. Being honest about your feelings or needs and your child's needs requires you to make sure your child goes to school and is not allowed to play in the street. An appropriate response using the child-centered approach you have been practicing in the situations described would be, "I know you don't want to go to school today, but it's time for going to school. When you get home today you can tell me all about it and do some fun things you want to do." If your child wanted to play in the street and didn't respond to limits, you could use choice-giving saying, "If you choose not to play inside the fence, you are choosing not to get to play outside with your friends. If you choose to play inside the fence, you are choosing to get to play outside with your friends."

If you practiced only the first two conditions ("I love you no matter what" and "I'll see the world through your eyes") without the third ("I'll be honest") in a situation where your child wanted to sleep with you every night, you would likely focus on what your child wanted or what you wanted rather than focus on what you both need. What you need is uninterrupted sleep, time with yourself or your spouse, and your own bedtime associated with your needs. If you focus on meeting this need, you will also be meeting your child's needs to learn to self-soothe and cope. Learning to sleep on his or her own will also lead to better sleep for your child. If your children learn how to go to sleep by you being in the room or cuddling them, then when they wake up in the middle of the night, they likely will not be able to go back to sleep without you there. If they sleep with you all night, then it's likely your bedtime will be their bedtime, but they have different sleep needs than you do.

To be focused on the child's needs or to be child centered means to set limits for the child. As stated earlier, students in a child-centered play therapy program were more likely to set limits than those who weren't in the program.[3] To relinquish parental authority or your own needs is to neglect the needs of your child. Children who are in charge of the family most likely experience feeling overwhelmed, as though there is no one to take care of them. They become impossible to manage, because their emotional needs are not being met.

To leave out any of the three conditions will make it impossible to act compassionately. For example, sometimes we practice the last condition of "I'll be honest" without practicing the other two conditions of "I love you no matter what" and "I'll see the world through your eyes." This type of "honesty" is what people call "brutal honesty." It may also take the form of blaming. For example, if you are frustrated with your husband because you think he's not doing enough around the house and you practice the third condition without the other two, you might say something like "You never do anything around here. I have to do it all myself." With this type of "honesty," you put the responsibility for your feelings on the other person, rather than taking responsibility for your own feelings. To practice all three of the conditions while being honest would sound something like this: "I feel overwhelmed. I don't know how I can get everything done that needs to be done. I need your help." This type of honesty requires you to take responsibility for your feelings and to be vulnerable. When you make the other person vulnerable, but not yourself, you are not practicing compassionate or true honesty. It's also important to recognize that compassionate honesty is more likely to evoke a harmonious response than "brutal or blaming" honesty.

One way to make sure you're following the three conditions is to notice if you are energized or drained by your relationships. Believe it or not, practicing compassion creates energy. Practicing anything else drains you. That is because trying to get others to be who you want them to be is draining. Even if you are trying to get them to be something better, such as a straight-A student or responsible or drug free, it will drain you because your intention is to change the person rather than love that person the way he or she is. This is not to say that you shouldn't set limits or have consequences for bad grades, acting irresponsibly, or doing drugs. It is the intention behind the consequences that matters. You intention is to meet the other person's needs, not make them into the person you want them to be.

The intention dramatically changes the dynamic of the relationship. For example, if my child comes home to tell me she has a bad grade and I am focused on who I want her to be, I may use controlling methods such as shaming or fear to make her a better student. I create a power struggle in which I act as though I am in a battle against my child to try to get her to be the person I think she should be. If instead I focus on acting compassionately, I implement consequences for bad grades in a loving way. I can empathize with my child's frustration and sadness over the bad grades and the consequences. I have created a situation in which I am struggling *with* my child, not *against* her.

You may have begun to notice the seemingly subtle differences between a healthy relationship and an unhealthy one. I say *seemingly* subtle, because although the shift seems like a minor one, it has profound consequences. Instead of controlling your feelings or letting them control you, you neither hold onto them nor push them away. You use your emotions as your guide, not as your master. Instead of holding onto them, you let them unfold. Instead of talking yourself out of them, you let them go when they have taught you what you need to know. You may also have noticed that your relationship with yourself is a reflection of your relationship with your child. Instead of controlling your children, you guide them. Instead of evaluating or praising your children, you value and prize them. While some of the words and phrases you use might be exactly the same, your intention has changed. You are no longer trying to make your child into someone you think he or she should be. Whatever you say is a reflection of your love for your child, a desire to see the world through his or her eyes, to understand him or her on the deepest possible level.

Everyone Matters

Every person deserves to be loved, just for being alive. Much of our behavior is an attempt to matter to others or to be loveable, because we don't know that we matter or are loveable just the way we are. I experienced this problem at a pre-internship site during my training to become a psychologist. While most pre-internships had gone smoothly for me, at one particular site I had a difficult time with the way my supervisor perceived me. Her words seemed to narrowly define who I was, not just as a therapist but also as a person. As I longed for someone who could make room for all of me, I realized that most of us, including myself, only see a very small part of each other. In fact, the only person I could think of who had not even seemed tempted to limit his perception of me was Garry Landreth, so I went to him for help.

As I explained my situation, he deftly reflected, "It seems as though you are upset by the way the people there are seeing you."

"Yes," I admitted. "I don't understand why they see me the way they do."

"You're used to being appreciated for your work," he reflected again. "Isn't it okay for them to see you any way they want to?" he asked.

With those words it seemed as though a whole new world opened up for me. I had spent so much energy—not just at this particular place but throughout my whole life—trying to control and change others' perceptions of me, believing that their perception somehow defined me. I began to realize that no one's perception of me could define me, not even my own. I began to imagine, though, that if I could know everyone's perception who had ever lived or who would ever live of one person or one thing, that I would know that person or thing's true reality. This led me to the realization that every person's perception of me was true. I am all that people see in me. Instead of seeing their perceptions as confining, I began to see them as an incredible opportunity.

For two days I lived with the knowledge that each person was a great gift to me. Whatever someone saw in me, good or bad, gave me a chance to build a relationship with that aspect they made real in me through their perception. Every human being on the planet could help me know myself and life more deeply as I built a relationship with them. It didn't matter how much they had achieved, how much they had evolved, how tolerant they had become, how much therapy they had, how educated they were—every single human being was intrinsically valuable to every other human being, and so was I. I did not have to prove that I had the right to exist. I understood, not just intellectually but emotionally, how valuable we all are to each other. I also experienced everyone as part of me and myself as part of everyone. I belonged wherever I was, just as everyone else did. After a couple of days, the knowledge I had gained began to fade, because I began to judge myself and others. While I understand this concept intellectually, emotionally I still struggle with it because of my need to evaluate. I will not be able to benefit from this knowledge until I understand it well enough to let go of evaluation. If I try to make myself stop evaluating, I am caught up again in trying to be who I think I'm supposed to be. I can change my behavior and stop using evaluative language, but I can't control my feelings or my desire to evaluate. I have to sit with those feelings until they reveal all they have to teach me. When I no longer need them, I will be able to let them go.

Let Your Children Know They Matter

One of my favorite ways to remind my children how much they matter to me is to write notes to them. Remember not to praise or evaluate in your note. Instead, write a "prizing" note that explains one of your child's strengths. For example, write a note saying "You got up and went to school today even though you were afraid too—that shows you're brave." Another great note for children who have trouble being organized might be: "You put all of your homework in the right binder pockets before you left for school today; that shows you're organized." Remember that your child has all the strengths that a human being can possibly have. Point them out so that they can see them.

Children especially love receiving notes in the mail. It only takes a little extra time to put a stamp on a note and address it to your child. Be sure to let your child retrieve the note from the mailbox. Notes are more special too when they're hidden in lunchboxes or under pillows. Kids love surprises.

Review of Previous Homework

What did you discover about yourself this week by practicing the "You are all you see in others" exercise? Have you noticed yet that the more you do this exercise, the less threatening and more fun it becomes, especially if you remember to practice fascination when you do it?

Homework[4]

1. Identify one of your child's strengths and write it down in a note. Hide it somewhere where he will find it. Identify another one of your child's strengths and mail a note to him.
2. Have another play session. Record and evaluate it.

9

FACILITATING YOUR CHILD'S HEALING

> **Survival Tip 9**
>
> Perfection Leads Away
> From Happiness,
> While Acceptance
> Leads You Toward It

By now you have started using the play therapy skills you've learned outside of the play session. The more you use reflective listening and ACT with the three conditions of a healthy relationship (I love you no matter what; I'll see the world through your eyes; I'll be honest) the more harmony you will create in your relationships. However, you may benefit even more with a little fine-tuning of the process. If you're feeling stuck or just wishing you could take things to the next level, this chapter is for you. Regardless of how things are going now, it's important to go back and review chapters 1 and 4. You will see them in a completely different way if you have been practicing special playtime for a few weeks.

As I've said many times before, the model you have been learning is designed to shift the way you relate to your child and the problems your child has. Most parents have the realization at some point during the program what role they have been playing that perpetuates their child's difficult behavior. Some patterns of relating, though, are so ingrained that they are difficult to change. For example, in most of the families I see and even in my own, one parent is too permissive while the other is too strict or harsh. The problem with this is that neither parenting style meets the emotional needs of the child.

I have noticed that permissive parents who have learned to use this model may fall into old permissive patterns that don't meet the child's needs by thinking that they can only reflect without setting limits, while overly strict or harsh parents who have learned this model may stay in their old patterns by using choice-giving too often (generally speaking, more than once a week) without using reflective listening, ACT, or having play sessions. While this comes a little closer to meeting the child's needs, it still may not be enough to create the harmony that you're craving. It's important to look at some of the underlying issues related to your parenting style.

Both permissive and harsh parenting styles are perpetuated by fear. Parents who are permissive are afraid of hurting or damaging their child, while parents who are harsh are afraid of being humiliated or embarrassed by their child. Permissive parents tend to try to rescue their children, while harsh parents try to control them. Some parents bounce back and forth between these two styles of parenting. Permissive parents often become so overwhelmed by trying to make their child happy or feel good about themselves and not being able to that they just blow up at their child. Harsh parents sometimes feel overwhelmed with guilt about being too hard on their children and try to make up for it by being permissive.

Because children who have one permissive parent and one harsh one usually lack coping skills, they often act in ways that are embarrassing for parents and so the parents bounce back and forth between being afraid of hurting their child's self-esteem and being afraid of what others will think of their parenting skills or their child. The different styles of parenting in the same family also seem to perpetuate each other. The permissive parent is permissive to make up for the overly strict, harsh parent and vice versa.

A family I have been working with taught me that when parents are stuck in these patterns it is usually a result of perfectionism. The mother, Shelley, was a stay-at-home mom who worried a lot about her daughters, Emily and Diana. She particularly worried about their self-esteem and emotional well-being. She was so overwhelmed by trying so hard to do everything just right that she had trouble enjoying being with her children. She dreaded holidays and summertime because the children were home with her all day. It wasn't that she didn't love her children, she just didn't know how to cope with her own emotions when they became emotional. When her children became upset or difficult to deal with, she felt like she had failed as a mother. Instead of setting limits, she tried too hard to make her children feel better.

The father, Bill, was a successful, hardworking perfectionist who thought his kids just needed to be whipped into shape. He was really irritated about therapy and often dismissed its value during our time together. He believed that old-fashioned methods that emphasized respect were best. He did not worry about his children fearing him as long as they behaved appropriately. However, the problem was that no matter how strict or demanding he was, his children's behavior did not improve.

While Shelley was trying to be the perfect parent, Bill was trying to make sure their children were perfect. Shelly was reluctant to set limits because she believed that if she were the perfect mother, she would always say just the right thing to make her children feel good about themselves. Bill was reluctant to connect emotionally because he didn't want to give up his perceived power over his children. Shelley felt that things weren't working because no matter how hard she tried, her daughters still had days when they felt like failures or thought they were fat when they weren't or complained a lot. Bill thought that things weren't getting better because no matter how hard he tried, his daughters still fought with each other, made messes they forgot to pick up, and got mad when they didn't get their way.

No matter how well your emotional needs are met, though, you are always going to have days when you feel like a failure or act irresponsibly. This method does not rid your child of problems; there is no method to do that. It teaches you how to relate in a therapeutic way to your child when there are problems. If you try to use these methods to perfect yourself or your children, you will end up in the same dysfunctional patterns that led you to pick up this book.

Author Pema Chödrön tells a story about how we often confuse deeper understanding with the idea of struggling to get from one bank of the river to the other. However, reaching a level of deeper understanding is more akin to floating in the middle of the river, between the two banks. It is acceptance of who we are, rather than striving to be perfect, that allows us to connect in a deeper way.[1]

Sometimes children get stuck in dysfunctional patterns. When children are stuck, it shows in their play sessions. One way children may communicate this is by trying to entertain you throughout the entire session. Usually when this happens, you will find yourself feeling as though you should laugh because you know your child wants you to, but you don't really feel the urge to laugh. The sessions will usually become boring too, because your child is preventing you from making a connection on a deeper level.

This happened with a client I was seeing, Toby, a 10-year-old boy who was having difficulty with anger outbursts at school. Occasionally, when circumstances are severe or children seem stuck, I see them for play sessions while their parents are also doing play sessions with them. I decided to see Toby for sessions because, although his parents were doing sessions with him, he seemed to repeat the same play over and over; although the frequency of his anger outbursts had diminished, they still occurred.

Toby was unusually smart. He excelled at all subjects academically but struggled socially. He had once become so angry on the playground that he kicked a boy hard, in the shins. He had also thrown his books on the floor in anger and yelled at his teachers. He had been suspended a couple of times and was eventually recommended for an alternative school program. Often he became so angry at school that he cried. His parents were worried that if the problems were not resolved he would become a social outcast in junior high.

During sessions, Toby did not want to talk about or play out anything that bothered him; instead, he tried to entertain me and make me laugh. I felt pressured to laugh out of politeness but eventually realized that this kept Toby from dealing with the real issues he struggled with. Using the three conditions of a healthy relationship as my guide, I realized that I was not being honest by continuously pretending something was funny when it wasn't. The next time Toby began to tell jokes, I reflected, "I noticed that you are always trying to make me laugh when you're in here." He responded by saying, "Yeah, I'm a funny guy. What can I say?" I reflected again saying, "It's really important to you that I'm enjoying our time together. You want me to be entertained. Entertaining me also means you don't have to talk about the things that bother you."

As our session progressed, I could simply smile and say, "You're trying to make me laugh again" instead of pretending to laugh when something wasn't funny to me. This eventually had an impact on Toby's behavior. He began to play with some of the figures I had in the playroom. One was a Zeus figure that children identified as God and the other was a Hercules figure. As he began a dialogue between the figures, he described God's disappointment with Hercules. No matter how hard Hercules tried, he kept making mistakes, usually ones he had no control over—like slipping off a mountain or tripping over something he didn't see.

I reflected Hercules' struggle by saying, "He's trying so hard to do what God wants him to do, but he just can't seem to do it." I further reflected, "Maybe you feel that way sometimes."

"What way?" he asked.

"Like no matter how hard you try, you can't do it right."

"Yeah," he responded.

I theorized out loud a little further. "Maybe you feel like God is disappointed in you."

He nodded his head and looked out into space thoughtfully.

"You've made some mistake you can't forgive yourself for," I reflected further.

He looked down and said, "I'm afraid God can't forgive me."

"I wonder what you did that you think God can't forgive you for," I said.

"I can't tell you," he responded.

"You don't have to tell me, but it might help if you did," I said.

"There's no way I'm going to tell you, even if it would help," he said.

I reflected, "It's really hard to talk about." I then asked him, "What does your family believe about mistakes and forgiveness?"

He answered, "They believe you should pray and ask God for forgiveness."

"Have you tried that?" I asked.

"No," he said, "I'm afraid to."

"Maybe you can try praying to God this week and ask him for help or ask him for forgiveness," I suggested, "or maybe you can talk to your mom and dad about this."

"I can't talk to my mom and dad because they will just want to know what I did, but I'll try to pray," he said.

During the next session Toby told me that he could not muster the courage to pray to God. I asked him if he thought God knew about the mistake he made and he said that he knew that God knew but felt too ashamed to talk about it. As the session continued, he began to reveal more with the God and Hercules figures.

I reflected on his play out loud, "It seems like one of the things that Hercules gets so mad about is that he can't be perfect. It also seems like God wants him to be perfect. Is that what's going on with you, Toby?"

"What do you mean?" he asked.

"Do you think you're supposed to be perfect or that God wants you to be perfect?" I asked.

He responded, "I don't know, maybe." Toby felt that he should try again to pray to God but was afraid he wouldn't be able to.

During the next session Toby explained again that he still couldn't bring himself to pray to God, and his play with the God and Hercules figures continued. Just as before, Hercules tried really hard to be perfect and do what God wanted him to do.

I theorized out loud, "Maybe you get up every morning and say to yourself, 'Today I'm not going to blow up or make any mistakes,' and then when you do make a mistake, because all of us do every day, you feel hopeless and defeated and blow up—not because you're mad at your teacher or the kids, but at yourself for not being able to be perfect."

"Yeah!" he said, "that's what I do!"

I reflected, "So your problem really is that you try too hard to be good, when what you really need to do is just be more forgiving when you make a mistake."

"How do I do that?" he wondered out loud.

"Well, let's see. When was the last time you blew up?"

He explained that the last time he blew up he was in the lunchroom and someone cut in line in front of him. When he confronted the boy politely, being careful not to blow up, a girl beside him said, "Oh, here we go again, Toby's going to make a scene." Imagine how frustrating it would be to try so hard and still be seen as the problem, when it was someone else who had broken the rules.

I reflected to Toby, "You're feeling like no matter what you do, people are always going to see you the same way." As we discussed and role-played different scenarios about how he might handle the situation, Toby came up with solutions he liked. One solution was to say to the girl, "Hey, sometimes I blow up and make a scene, but not this time." The other solution Toby liked was using his sense of humor by saying "You say that like there's something wrong with that. I'm not a psycho (making funny faces and contortions with his body)."

The next time I saw Toby, he couldn't wait to tell me that he had prayed to God and asked for forgiveness. He told his parents, too, how hard he had been trying to be perfect and how he had struggled to pray to God. Remarkably, Toby had no anger outbursts for the next 4 months. Even more remarkable was his recovery after the blowup. He apologized and made fun of himself much in the same way we had role-played. His teachers began to notice the change and commented to his mother. One of his teachers wrote a note complimenting Toby on how much he had grown.

It's ironic that striving to be better or trying so hard not to make a mistake could make things worse. How often have we said to our kids "Try your hardest" or "Do your best," not realizing that we may be setting a trap for them. When children are praised and criticized, they may start to disown the parts of themselves they believe to be "bad." Just like Toby, they try so hard to be only the "good" without any "bad" that it contributes to their behavior problems.

Play Themes

When children are struggling with something it shows up in their play. You can identify the themes in your child's play by closely observing the language, behaviors, and patterns expressed. Some examples of play themes include good versus evil, power and control, nurturing, loss, fears and phobias, trust and betrayal, testing limits, mastery, and competence. The possibilities are probably infinite.

Some themes are obvious. For example, when the army men are attempting to slay the giant fire-breathing dragon, that's probably good versus evil. If your child is tying you up and handcuffing you, it could mean he is working on issues of power and control or it could mean he wants to feel attached to you. Sorting or ordering the money or toys could be an expression of mastery or competency. However, money play could also represent themes of trust. When your child is cooking or taking care of the baby or you, it may mean she is playing out nurturing themes. Checking out your heart with the stethoscope may be a nurturing theme or a trust theme. Playing store may also be an expression of your child trying to build trust with you. Games of skill or games in which the child makes sure that she wins could be an expression of your child wanting to feel competent and in control.

The way to understand the themes of your child's play is to imagine what it feels like to play what your child is playing. Imagine what would inspire you to play with the toys that way or what feelings it might soothe to play the way in which your child is playing. It's also important to consider what the child doesn't do. As Dr. Landreth states:

☞ What a child doesn't do is as important as what the child does.[2]

For example, if the child leaves out a particular family member in the dollhouse play, doesn't face you during playtime, or won't let the dollhouse dolls play on the second floor of the dollhouse because there are no stairs to the second floor, these are all important considerations about what the child's play is about.

Perhaps the most difficult thing to remember when you do understand a theme is that you don't have to fix anything. The play themes are not problems to be fixed, they are windows into your child's world. In fact, if you try to fix anything, you will more than likely make the feelings unconscious and take away the child's place to work on the issues he is expressing. The purpose of understanding the themes is simply to help the parent see the world through the child's eyes.

When a child's play in the session changes in some way, it is usually a sign that the child has worked something out. Remember that behavior problems in the play session could mean that the child views the play session as a safe place to work out issues. The behavior may get worse in the play session before it gets better.

Helping Your Child Move On

William, a child I worked with whom I have mentioned earlier in the book, seemed to be stuck in play sessions, playing the same thing over and over. He had one figure he called the "good guy" and one who was the "cool guy." The cool guy got in trouble and misbehaved a lot, while the good guy kept trying to do the right thing. William created opposite situations for them. When one had a blue room with a red bed, the other would have a red room with a blue bed. If one wore blue pants with a red shirt, the other wore a red shirt with blue pants. He played out this theme for several months and seemed stuck. I decided during a family session to use a technique taught by Violet Oaklander that she called the "Fairy Godmother" technique.[3]

Giving Your Child Fairy Godparents

During the session, William's mother began to explain that William believed it when other children told him he was ugly and so she then tried to convince him that he was "good looking." When William resisted, I reflected that sometimes he didn't like certain things about himself. I then told him I had an idea and asked if he would participate. He agreed and I asked him to think of a part of himself he didn't like. He said he couldn't think of anything, and his mother happily commented that he must like everything about himself. I reflected her feelings but then explained that everyone had at least some part themselves they liked less than the rest of them. I then reflected William's feelings, explaining that maybe it was difficult to talk about the parts of himself he didn't like. I was quiet for a while, giving William time to struggle with his feelings, and then he said that he knew a part of himself that he didn't like, but he wouldn't talk about it. The following dialogue depicts the remainder of the session.

> *Therapist*: Hmmm, Okay, just pick out something in the room to be that part of yourself. Anything you want.
>
> *William*: (Picks out the Tyrannosaurus Rex puppet.)
>
> *Therapist*: Oh, you decided on that one. Okay. Now choose a puppet to be your fairy godmother.
>
> *William*: (Moves toward an object then stops abruptly, looking stumped.)
>
> *Therapist*: Looks like you're trying to decide.
>
> *William*: Uh, well, can I have a fairy godfather?
>
> *Therapist*: Oh, sure. A fairy godfather, of course. You need a fairy godfather.
>
> *William*: Okay. Here. (Picks out a Stegosaurus puppet.)
>
> *Therapist*: Okay. Now I want you to put on a puppet show for me and use this part of yourself and the fairy godfather.
>
> *William*: Okay. (He is ready to start right away.)
>
> *Therapist*: But there's one thing. Remember, the fairy godfather loves him (pointing to T. Rex), no matter what. That's how fairy godfathers are. They always love you no matter what.
>
> *William*: (Stops suddenly and is very quiet for a while. Looks as though he is struggling with the idea. Walks the T. Rex puppet into the sandbox and then takes him out.) I can't do it.

Therapist: It's hard to imagine. Just remember, he loves him no matter what. It doesn't matter what he does. He loves him.

William: (Is silent for a while then moves T. Rex to the sandbox and T. Rex begins to terrorize the grandmother and kill people and throw them around. Then he walks the fairy godfather into the sandbox and says in a loving and nurturing voice.) You have made many bad choices and now you will have to pay the consequences. You have to control yourself or you will keep getting in trouble, and I don't want that to happen to you. (The fairy godfather walks away and the T. Rex goes back to destroying the people and their things. William comes over to me and says…) He won't change. He keeps doing it.

Therapist: Yeah, I know, but the fairy godfather loves him no matter what. He needs to know that.

William: (Starts to walk the fairy godfather back over to the sandbox then stops to whisper to me…) But he is the devil! (He looks at me wide-eyed, waiting for a response.)

Therapist: Oh, I see. That part of you is the devil. But the fairy godfather still loves him. He loves him, no matter what.

William: (Takes the T. Rex and begins to destroy everything again. Then he walks the fairy godfather over to T. Rex.)

Therapist: He needs to hear the fairy godfather tell him.

William: (He looks at me and then at the puppets and has the fairy godfather speak) I love you, no matter what. (The T. Rex begins to pick up the old lady, the children, and the car and cares for them. Then he looks up at me silently for a while.)

Therapist: Something happened to him. He's different now.

William: He wasn't really bad.

Therapist: Hmmm. He just needed to know his fairy godfather loved him.

William: He just needed to know someone cared about him. That's all he ever needed.

His mother was very moved by what William had done, and so was I. It seemed as though he had connected with something inside himself that he hadn't had access to before. During the next session, William's dollhouse play changed dramatically. He stacked the beds on top of each other and moved the boys into the same room. The opposite-mirroring had disappeared. He made several different rooms for the boys and used every floor of the house. He made special places where they could play, eat, listen to music, and sleep. The boys moved around freely on every floor and he made a room for his mother, whom he said was very lonely. William's behavior also changed dramatically outside the playroom, and within weeks he moved for the first time in his life to a regular classroom.

If your child is stuck, you might try the technique illustrated above. It doesn't always work as well as it did in that example. I've noticed in my own practice that it works best after I have been doing play sessions for a while—at least 6 months. If your child does not feel safe enough to be vulnerable in the play sessions, it's not likely he will do this with you. If it's not really what the child needs, he also won't do it, so don't push this technique too hard. As always, focus more on what unfolds than on what you want the outcome to be.

Structured Doll Play

Another technique that can be very helpful for children who are having a difficult time with a particular situation is "Structured Doll Play."[2] Structured doll play involves making up a story that helps a child understand what to expect in a particular situation. This is an especially helpful technique to use with children between the ages of 2 and 6 when they seem to feel anxious about something. In my practice I use it most often with children who need to have surgery or with kids who are nervous about visiting a noncustodial parent. I have also used it with kids who have a fear of shots or visits to the dentist and those who have separation anxiety when it's time to go to school or to the babysitter. Parents may want to use this technique to explain divorce to young children.

The first and most important step is to imagine all of the things that might be scary or difficult for a child in the situation you will be acting out. Not knowing what to expect is scary for most of us, but kids may have other fears such as "Will I get hurt?" or "Will the kids/teacher/babysitter be mean?" Other more serious fears such as "Will Mommy/Daddy come back?" or "Will Mommy/Daddy still love me and take care of me?" may also need to be considered. You won't mention any of these fears in the story, but it is important as always to see the world through the child's eyes. As you tell the story, you are showing the child how to behave rather than how to feel, so you won't talk about the feelings at all.

You may begin the story by having your child pick out all of the necessary players as described in the fairy godfather story above (for example, pick out something in the room to be you. Okay, now pick out something to be your teacher, and so forth) or you can pick out the players you need ahead of time. It's important to use figures, dolls, or stuffed animals to represent the characters in the story, because it helps the child process the information if he can see it acted out.

Start with a familiar, predictable part of the child's life. For example, if the issue is going to school, start with waking up with a hug and having breakfast together. Making lots of sound effects (an alarm clock sound when it's time to get up; a frying egg sound while you make breakfast) and using lots of personal details (Johnnie was wearing his favorite rocket ship pajamas; he sat on three pillows and a phone book just like he did every morning) makes the story more interesting and enjoyable. In the middle of the story tell the part the child is afraid of, remembering to focus on details that will be familiar to him like getting into the car and buckling the seat belt and listening to the radio or his favorite CD, and seeing his best friend, Chase, walking into the school. Rather than focusing on the problem, focus on the necessary behaviors the child goes through to accomplish the task; for example, giving Mom a hug and kiss good-bye, closing the car door with a big slam (don't forget to make a sound effect), opening the big glass door, waving hello to Mrs. Johnson, putting his books in his locker (another opportunity for sound effects), and sitting down at his desk. The end of the story should include the resolution, most likely the fact that you will be back to pick him up and listen to what happened during his day and help him with anything he needs help with. If there is something that your child may look forward to after the ordeal, such as a cartoon or his favorite after-school snack, put that in the story too.

Don't put anything in the story that you don't have control over. For example, don't say that your child made all As or that no one will be mean to him. Also don't talk about emotions you have, such as missing your child. Instead, you can say, "Mommy was thinking about Johnnie while she worked and Johnnie was thinking about Mommy while he was at school." When you tell the story remember to use third person, saying the child's name and "Mommy" or "Daddy" instead of "you" or "me." The point of the story is to help the child feel more secure about knowing what to expect and having some idea about what is going to happen.

Structured Doll Play for Loss and Trauma

Another time this technique may be used is when your child has suffered a loss of some kind or has been abused or traumatized. In these types of cases, the story is used to give the child the message "It's not your fault." You may be wondering why a child who has lost a parent or been abused or traumatized might think it's his fault. Before the age of 7 most children don't have the ability to think logically. Their reasoning is based mostly on the idea that things that occur at the same time cause each other. For example, when Daddy goes to work in the morning, he gets into the car—therefore, the car is taking my daddy away and I hate the car. Until the age of 7, children also have a difficult time taking someone else's perspective, so if there is a problem, they usually feel it is something they did. For example, if parents get a divorce, children may think it's something they did. If Mommy is crying, it's their fault. If Daddy is mad, it's because they were thinking something they shouldn't have been thinking.

It's also important to realize that when children experience a loss or trauma of some kind, it's likely they may regress to a previous developmental level. They may not be able to reason or think logically after the event has occurred; if they are overwhelmed by the event, it may be easier to think it is their fault than to believe the event is something they have no control over.

When you tell the story, you tell the events that happened as you know them in the third person. In this type of story you can talk about the child's feelings, saying, "I think maybe Johnnie was feeling scared, or maybe just really mad. I'm not sure." Don't talk about your own feelings, though, unless your child saw you crying, too. If he did, say, "Mommy was crying, but it wasn't Johnnie's fault. It was nothing Johnnie did. Sometimes grown-ups get sad, too." As you wrap up the story say, "Johnnie thought it was all his fault, but it wasn't. None of this was Johnnie's fault. His mommy and daddy held him and told him 'It's not your fault, Johnnie.'"

Sand Play

If you're struggling with control issues in your sessions with your child, it may be helpful to add a box of sand to your special play-time. It's important to point out, however, how messy sand can be. Some parents have substituted a box of beans for sand so that the mess is more manageable. In my experience, though, when the child is stuck in a very controlling mode (for example, when he says, "You put this on that one. No, not that way, like this. You didn't do it right, you have to put that one on this side."), the sand often works to shift the play.

Quite often a child who is controlling the play has felt controlled by the parent. The sand introduces a level of loss of control for the parent that is therapeutic for the parent and the child. Adding sand may also work well for children who restrict their play to themes of mastery and competency. This is another way to control the sessions. Staying in mastery play for the entire session or for several sessions may indicate that the child is afraid to feel vulnerable in the session.

If you choose to add sand to the playtime, I recommend using a large vinyl tablecloth to put under the sandbox. An under-the-bed plastic box with a lid makes a wonderful special playtime sandbox. Although you can expect that at least a little sand will get out of the box, remember to set limits using ACT. For example, "I know you want to play with the sand over there, but the sand is for staying in the box, you can bring that toy over to the sandbox if you wish." Although you would rarely use choice-giving during special playtime, sand play may make it necessary. For example, if you've used ACT three times and your child still tries to take the sand out of the box, you can say, "If you choose to take the sand out of the box, you are choosing not to get to play with the sand. If you choose to keep the sand in the box, you are choosing to get to play with the sand. Which do you choose?"

Frequently Asked Questions

Below is a list of frequently asked questions[2] about common problems parents have with play sessions. See if you have mastered the material enough to answer them.

1. My child notices that I talk differently in the play sessions and wants me to talk normally. What should I do?
2. My child asks many questions during the play sessions and resents my not answering them. What should I do?
3. My child just plays and has fun. What am I doing wrong?
4. I'm bored. What's the value of this?
5. My child doesn't respond to my comments. How do I know I'm on target?
6. When is it okay for me to ask questions, and when is it not okay?
7. My child hates the play sessions. Should I discontinue them?
8. My child wants the playtime to be longer. Should I extend the session?
9. My child wants to play with the toys at other times during the week. Is that okay?
10. My child wants me to shoot at her during the play session. What should I do?

Answers to Frequently Asked Questions

Compare your answers to the ones below.

1. *My child notices that I talk differently in the play sessions and wants me to talk normally. What should I do?*

Reflect your child's feelings, "You noticed I'm talking differently." You can also explain why you are talking differently by saying, "Talking this way helps me see the world through your eyes. It helps me understand how you feel." You probably feel awkward. You may want to work more on conveying interest ("I am here, I hear and see you, I understand, I care") with your responses and your facial expressions.

2. *My child asks many questions during the play sessions and resents my not answering them. What should I do?*

The purpose of not answering questions is to return responsibility to the child. If you give your child the answers, she doesn't have the opportunity to experience her own wisdom. However, some questions may be answered. For example, if your child asks a question such as, "You went shopping yesterday, didn't you, Mommy?" you wouldn't respond with, "You're wondering if I went shopping yesterday." Instead, you would respond with, "You remembered that!" answering the question in essence but not in a way that makes you the expert.

3. *My child just plays and has fun. What am I doing wrong?*

Nothing. Your child is supposed to use the time however he wants.

4. *I'm bored. What's the value of this?*

The message you send by simply being there is extremely valuable because you have put aside your own needs for your child's. It might be valuable to explore your feelings of boredom (see chapter 7).

5. *My child doesn't respond to my comments. How do I know I'm on target?*

Usually when you are on target, your child will let you know. If she doesn't respond to a reflection, you may want to explore other feelings she might be having or convey that you're trying to understand. For example if you have reflected "You really are angry" and your child doesn't respond, you might add, "or maybe it's not anger you're feeling. Maybe you're just feeling really strong and powerful." If your child still doesn't respond you might say, "Maybe that's not it either. I wonder what it could be that you're feeling."

6. *When is it okay for me to ask questions, and when is it not okay?*

Remember, the general rule of thumb is, "If you have enough information to ask a question, you have enough information to make a statement." Instead of asking, "Are you feeling sad?" simply state, "You're sad." Instead of asking "How are you feeling?" simply comment, "I wonder how you're feeling right now." The reason statements are usually better than questions is because children usually feel pressured by our questions. They don't always tell you how they feel; instead, they may tell you what they know you want to hear or if they don't know what you want to hear, they may shut down. All of that said, a question here or there won't destroy a relationship. If you can't think of any other way to find out what you need to know, ask. Try to convey the question, though, in a way that communicates your openness to the answer.

7. *My child hates the play sessions. Should I discontinue them?*

No, don't discontinue them. Your child can use the play session any way he wants to and is free to use them in a way that he enjoys. Always try to see the world through his eyes, though. Does he hate the session because it is scheduled during his favorite TV program or because he has to stop doing something he is enjoying? If this is the case, instead of changing the playtime, you may want to use this opportunity to help your child develop coping skills to handle not getting what he wants exactly when he wants it. Reflect your child's feelings about hating the play session and say that he can talk about how much he hates the play session for the entire time if he wants to. You may also want to practice limit-setting, saying, "I know you don't want to have a special playtime right now, but it's time for our special playtime. I'll record your show and when our special playtime is over, then you can watch it." If you're not sure why your child doesn't want to have special playtime, you may still reflect, set limits, or try suggesting that he try it for 10 minutes.

8. *My child wants the playtime to be longer. Should I extend the session?*

No. Sticking to the length you have decided is extremely important because it sets a limit. Use this as an opportunity to reflect your child's feelings and build her coping skills. You can still spend time with her doing fun things together or listening to her after the session, just be sure to set the limit on special playtime.

9. *My child wants to play with the toys at other times during the week. Is that okay?*

No. The toys are only used for special playtime. If the child is allowed to play with them anytime during the week, he may not be interested in having special playtime. The toys lose their "specialness" if they can be played with anytime. Use this as an opportunity to build coping skills.

10. *My child wants me to shoot at her during the play session. What should I do?*

Set the limit. For example, if your child says, "I'm the bad guy, shoot me," say, "I know you want me to shoot you, but people are not for shooting. I can pretend you're the bad guy getting away and catch you, or you can draw a picture of the bad guy getting shot."

What Are Your Questions?

You may have questions that haven't been answered. Try using the skills you've learned so far to answer them. If you still don't know the answer after you've tried reflective listening, ACT, choice-giving, and the three conditions for a healthy relationship, try visiting specialplaytime.com.

Review of Homework

Continue to hide and mail notes for your child to find. I used to put them in my daughter's lunchbox when she was in elementary school and she still has most of them. If you're artistic, draw a picture. If you're funny, make a joke. If you're poetic, write a poem. If you have no talent, don't worry. Your child won't notice that. Just let your child know that you are thinking about her or him.

Homework[2]

1. Give your child a "Sandwich Hug." A sandwich hug is when a child or children are hugged between two parents and the parents say, "We're the bread/sesame seed bun/Kaiser roll and you're the turkey/hamburger/ham." If you're a single parent, give your child a "burrito hug" using the same idea.
2. Have a play session with your child. Record it and evaluate it.

10
You Did It!

> **Survival Tip 10**
>
> **Be the Change You Want
> to See in Your Child**

What you might have noticed in practicing the methods in this book is that you have changed as much—if not more—than your child. Give yourself a pat on the back for all the hard work and self-reflection you have done.

It's time to look back at exactly what has changed since you started this program. Take the time to fill out the following questions. They are the same ones you filled out before you read this book. Don't look back at what you said when you started this program until you finish filling it out a second time.

Child Behavior Inventory

What are your child's strengths?

_____

_____

_____

What is your child's bedtime like?

_____

_____

_____

How is it getting your child up in the morning and ready to go somewhere?

_____

_____

_____

What is homework time like?

_____

_____

_____

What is it like when you ask your child to do chores?

_____

_____

_____

What are the problems you encounter when you take your child out in public?

_____

_____

_____

What disrespectful behaviors have you been tolerating (for example, yelling, ignoring, refusing to cooperate, hitting others, or saying hurtful things to others)?

_____

_____

_____

What is your child doing that is difficult for you to deal with (for example, giving up easily or not trying, throwing temper tantrums, or not taking responsibility for mistakes)?

_____

_____

_____

When do you find yourself overwhelmed with your child?

_____

_____

_____

What behaviors do you wish you could change in your child?

_____

_____

_____

Which of your child's feelings are most difficult for you to deal with?

_____

_____

_____

What is your biggest fear?

_____

_____

_____

How do you wish things could be with your child?

_____

_____

_____

Parent Behavior Inventory

What are your strengths?

_____

_____

_____

What do you do when your child will not cooperate with you?

_____

_____

_____

What do you do when your child misbehaves?

_____

_____

_____

What do you do when your child whines?

_____

_____

_____

What do you do when your child is demanding?

_____

_____

_____

What do you do when your child is angry?

_____

_____

_____

What do you do when your child is sad or crying?

_____

_____

_____

What do you do when you feel your child is manipulating you?

_____

_____

_____

What do you do when your child is disrespectful?

_____

_____

_____

What do you do when your child is helpless or his or her feelings are hurt?

_____

_____

_____

As you compare your answers now with the answers you wrote down before you read this book, ask yourself what has changed. Was it you or your child who changed the most? What behaviors have you changed and which ones has your child changed? Do you see your child differently? Does your child seem to see himself or you differently? What did you find out about your child's behaviors? What did you find out about your own intentions?

In situations where you struggled as a parent, not sure what to do, now you know exactly what to do. You know you can handle anything your child does with love, respect, and skill. No matter what the situation, if you empathize with your child and focus on what he or she needs (not wants) while using reflective responding, ACT, or choice-giving, you can't go wrong.

In addition to having the skills to handle any situation, you know how to be with your child in his feelings without rescuing him or shaming him for feeling the way he does. In this way, you have deepened your relationship with your child. Hopefully, you have more energy now because you aren't trying to make your child happy all of the time or trying to control your child. Instead, you are focused on guiding him or her in a loving but firm way.

As my trust in Dylan grew, so did his trust in me and our trust in ourselves. I began to enjoy being with Dylan again and looked forward to having playtime and other activities with him. We had a wonderful summer together, bike riding, exploring a nearby creek, and going to a nearby amusement park. Dylan worked very hard at his chores and was responsible for more than he ever had been. He and his sister also became close, and he began to be very nurturing toward her. Although he became angry occasionally and still yelled, he did not push or hit others anymore. He still showed no improvement in peer relationships but seemed content to stay at home and spend time with me and his sister.

Once school started, he began immediately to berate himself, calling himself stupid and saying that nobody liked him. He also had a couple of angry outbursts, but more often cried and felt sad about his problems at school. This behavior was due, at least in part, to Dylan's struggle with learning disabilities. His disabilities became much more apparent in the third grade, not only because the material was more difficult than the previous year but also because he had stopped masking his difficulties with hyperactive, defiant, or disruptive behavior. Dylan's third-grade teachers were also much more sensitive to his needs and behavior and recognized his problems immediately. They were extremely helpful in convincing the administration to have him tested. It was discovered during this process that Dylan had dyslexia. Although he was very frustrated by his disability, he experienced acceptance and understanding for the same behaviors he had been humiliated for during the previous year. During our playtime he began to reveal how he had been shamed and humiliated the previous year by his inability to do the work expected of him. He had believed that he was stupid and had devised elaborate cover-ups to hide his disability from the other children and the teachers. His behavior in the classroom changed dramatically as he began to feel accepted.

Recovery

Dylan began to thrive in ways my husband and I had hoped for. He began to make friends and was open to playing with children he had refused to play with before. Children started calling to see if he could come over or walk to school with them. They stopped by the house frequently and invited Dylan over to their homes. It seemed that several children liked Dylan and enjoyed his company and vice versa. He also began to play again during his play sessions with me. His play centered on good winning over evil, depicting a good monster devouring the bad guys and transforming them into good guys. He began to be able to admit his weaknesses and rely on his strengths, in particular, his creativity. He became flexible and willing to take risks appropriately. His soccer coach described him as the player who was willing to try every position and enjoyed participating and learning, even when he made mistakes.

Dylan also started sculpting beautiful abstract sculptures he imagined as "places for children." He described these places as fun and safe, pointing out the ways in which children would enjoy climbing, sliding, hiding, and playing with other children on them. The sculptures marked the beginning of Dylan's renewed enjoyment in pleasurable activities completely of his own initiative and his first serious attempt at sculpting. He was very proud of his sculptures and imagined one day making them large enough so that children really could enjoy them the way he envisioned. The artwork in his play sessions also began to change. He drew a house with trees (Figure 10.1) that was dramatically different from the house he drew just before play sessions began (Figure 10.2). The house has three chimneys, each one with a smaller puff of smoke than the last, seeming to imply a decrease in anger. The trees appear to be strong and healthy, unlike the scarred trees of his previous drawings. Dylan also liked to draw islands with palm trees (Figure 10.3), what Allan[1] describes as symbolic of ego strength.

After about 6 months of play sessions, Dylan's drawings reminded me of the rings of growth inside a tree (Figure 10.4). When I asked Dylan how it felt to draw them, he explained that his feeling depended on the color of the paper he drew on. When he drew on the yellow paper he felt excited and happy, and when he drew on the turquoise he felt peaceful and calm. The one I have included begins as a heart shape and emanates from the center, spreading out off the edges of the paper. He named this one "The Center." This drawing seems to symbolize the activation of the self-actualizing tendency.

Figure 10.1

My Personal Journey: What I Learned

Experiencing the remarkable changes that took place in my son and in our relationship has been a transforming experience for me and has developed in me a deep belief in a child's ability to heal. What became quickly apparent through these sessions was how my expectations of my son and disappointments in him affected him and our relationship. Much of my parenting behavior that I thought was motivated by my child's needs was instead a result of my own needs—or, rather, wants. It was only by rendering my expectations, disappointments, and needs powerless during our weekly play sessions that I was able to be aware of them. The play sessions provided my son a consistently safe and healthy environment that he could use as he most needed. They also provided me with the opportunity not only to become more aware of behaviors that impeded my own and my son's growth but also to function without those behaviors, thus breaking cycles, even generational cycles, of dysfunctional behavior. Because this is indeed a monumental task for any parent, I believe it is important that overly enthusiastic parents be required to restrict themselves to only one 30-minute session per week while in training.

Figure 10.2

Seeing the world through Dylan's eyes and giving him the support and freedom to express any of his feelings allowed me to once again experience the wonder of childhood; it also brought me face to face with Dylan's most painful feelings, the ways in which I had prevented him from healing, and my own childhood wounds. Initially, these feelings were so overwhelming that I was unable to experience them and instead found myself feeling bored during sessions. It took time and support to move through my feelings of loss and sadness, and it was only after that process that I was ready to be with my son in his struggle. This experience was reminiscent of childbirth, where I experienced resistance to pain, then finally totally surrendered to it, giving birth to a miracle. In this way, it seems to be a natural process, creating a rebirth of the self for the parent and the child.

Figure 10.3

Figure 10.4

My experience with my son was, of course, in many ways a much different experience than that of being a play therapist, but it helped me to develop in ways that I feel will benefit any client I see. This experience has also helped me to better empathize with and understand the parents I work with. I had used these techniques before with other clients and in certain situations with my own children, but

I had used them as a therapist or as I needed them—but not always when my son needed me to. What I have learned from this experience has affected all areas of my life. In the group I saw firsthand how feelings I reject in myself build a wall of shame internally and a wall of judgment and arrogance externally. I have learned to trust my feelings of rejection toward others as a guide to reclaiming that lost part of myself that they have brought to my attention. As I learned to allow Dylan and myself to express our true feelings, I learned to appreciate that our emotional experience is what guides us not just to a connection with each other but to the depths of our being and a connection to all that has been created.

I know that my son will still struggle and sometimes fail. I will still make mistakes that will deeply hurt him, and we will both experience painful feelings, but I no longer believe that to be healed means to never feel insecure or ashamed. Instead, I will strive to honor these feelings as an important part of us. Through this experience I have learned to value wholeness more than healing, allowing myself to embrace that part of me that will always be wounded.

I have also come to know that finding my place in the world does not require me to be better or the best; in fact, those strivings have gotten in the way of belonging. My place in the world is a tiny, infinitesimal point connecting me to a vast universe and was always just another part of me I only needed to allow myself to realize.

Dylan and I continued to have special playtime for many years. Sometimes we played, sometimes we talked. One special playtime, we spent the entire time howling and making strange noises. I was never sure what our time would be like. The world through my son's eyes unfolded and I just knew how lucky I was to be there with him.[2]

"Where Do I Go From Here?"

Parents ask me, "How long should I have special playtime with my kids?" I used to always answer, "Until their eighteenth birthday." Now that Dylan is 20 years old, I answer, "For the rest of their lives." Special playtime will change and develop as your child grows, but it will always be a time to connect with your child in much the same way you have learned in this book. For example, when they are 11 to 14 years old, you may want to include more art materials or projects they enjoy, but you will still be focused on seeing the world through their eyes, being with them in their feelings without fixing or rescuing them, and setting limits with ACT when appropriate. You may be surprised about where you end up. My special playtime with Dylan evolved into playing African drums together in a band! Deva and I take a kickboxing class together now. While I don't have the chance to use play therapy skills in either of these settings, these times became an important part of our relationship, time spent together, every week, having fun.

In both cases with my children, I was invited by them to join their activity. It's important that you make sure you're not interfering with an activity your child wants to do on his or her own. I think it might have been important, although maybe not intentional at the time, that my kids chose activities that they were better at than I am, and I will never surpass them in either of these areas no matter how hard I try.

In addition to the activities we chose, I was sure to use the play therapy skills regularly at home. As your children mature, you probably won't need toys. When Dylan was in his early teens and needed to talk to me about something that was bothering him, he would say, "Mom, I need a special playtime." We didn't have any toys or play with anything, but I would listen to his problems using the same skills I had in our playtime, practicing my faith in his ability to be guided by his own inner wisdom.

I also developed the habit of using the skills whenever there was a stressful situation. The skills became a safety net to use when tensions were high, buttons were pushed, or feelings were hurt. I wish I could say that I never reverted back to old behaviors, but I'm not sure that's even possible. What did happen is that the shaming, controlling behaviors became less and less prominent over time and I apologized for them when I did slip up. Also, my kids set limits on them, which is another important safety net to have. I want my kids to be able to protect themselves from my mistakes and others' mistakes.

It's really hard to tell what impact this has had on Dylan and Deva in the long term. I don't think I can take credit for who they have become, because the play therapy skills that became so central to their upbringing really emphasize faith in who they are, rather than shaping and molding them into who I wanted them to be. As I've said before, I see the skills I've learned as helping me learn how to stay out of their way so that they could develop into the people they were meant to be. The limits I set with them helped me to teach my children to stay out of their own way.

Have you noticed that sometimes you have trouble staying out of your own way? The wounded part of us will always take over if we don't take care of it. Whenever there are problems in someone's life that he or she has helped to create, it seems to be a result of the wounded part of that person being in control, making all of the decisions in his or her life. For example, whenever you find yourself shaming someone or trying to make him or her feel guilty, it is that part of you that feels ashamed or guilty that is calling the shots. When you don't take care of yourself, indulging your wants, instead of making sure you get what you need, the part of you that hasn't been nurtured is in control. It never works to beat yourself up. When you aren't able to harmonize with yourself or someone you love, it is a result of not knowing how to be compassionate with that wounded aspect in yourself or someone else.

It is when I see my children being compassionate that I am the most proud of them. Think about it. Is there anything more important that your child can be? When Dylan moved away to college, I thought his grades would be the most important measure of his success as a young adult, but I learned from him that he had much more to offer.

During our visits to see Dylan I noticed that he was saying "Hello" to people on the streets, people who were homeless. I would ask, "Who was that?" and he would tell me not just their names but also their stories. He had taken the time to listen to them and learn about them. I began noticing throughout our visits that when Dylan gave someone some change, they usually gave him something back. The most touching of these gifts was a drawing a man called Hawk made for him on the spot. Hawk took out a cherished canvas, one that someone had thrown away, a rare find even in the dumpsters behind the art classes at the college. He also had some paint pens that were covered with paints and dirt that had obviously been taken out of the trash. He began drawing triangular points that eventually I could recognize was a crown of thorns.

After one of our visits I was inspired by Dylan's compassion and decided to reach out to a homeless lady in front of a neighborhood grocery store. What I realized as I introduced myself and handed her the lemonade I had purchased for her at the store was that my rescue button was being pushed and I didn't know how to turn it off. In other words, I was not being compassionate, as I had intended, I was in a rescuing mode and couldn't seem to get out of it. As I thought back to Dylan's behavior, I realized that he knew something I didn't. First of all, he did not run up to all the homeless people he saw trying to make them feel better, he merely responded to their efforts to reach out to him. When I talked to him later and commented that I noticed the people he gave money to always gave him something back, he exclaimed, "No, not always, sometimes I have to ask them. Some people want to take advantage of me, but I don't let them get away with it." Since that conversation, I've realized that I'm not sure who is having special playtime with whom when we talk or visit with each other.

My daughter, Deva, has taught me a lot, too. She doesn't have dyslexia and by the time she was three I had learned how to be a skilled parent, so she didn't suffer the same way that Dylan did through my struggles to understand what I needed to do. Because she was so young when I began using the skills I've told you about in this book, I had the experience of using these skills with a child who hadn't yet learned to regulate her emotions. Quite honestly, it was pretty scary at times. I remember worrying that a child couldn't learn how to behave without shaming, controlling parents! In fact, there were times when I thought she was doing worse than other children. What I realized, though, was that she was just able to talk to me about all of her feelings. For example, whenever she felt insecure or unpopular or anything that we all go through at some point or another in our childhood, she could actually talk to me and even cry to me about it. What this meant, though, is that I had to really be with her in the pain she was experiencing a lot during her growing years. Although it was easier in many ways because I wasn't trying to rescue her, I was still requiring her to do chores and be responsible for everything she could be. In some ways it was much more difficult, because I had to develop my own emotional coping skills and self-control. Now that she is 15, I can say without hesitation that it was well worth it. She is the most motivated person I believe I have ever known. Can you imagine how easy that makes my job? I don't have to ask her to do her homework or worry about her grades. They are completely her responsibility because she is so motivated to learn and develop. She has pursued many of her interests and never half-heartedly. I believe it's because she is guided by her innate wisdom and talents rather then by who she thinks we want her to be. Her biggest struggle lately is trying to balance compassion and acceptance with protecting herself from kids her age who do things she doesn't believe would be good for her.

Something I've learned from both of my children is that it is better to let them tell you what they believe is right and wrong rather than for you to tell them. For example, when Deva's friend started smoking cigarettes, I worried about what she needed from me to be able to handle the situation, but she didn't need my help. She knew what to do. As she was walking the girl home from our house, she explained to her friend that she didn't want to smoke because she had opportunities that she didn't want to mess up. She also explained to her friend, "Those things kill you." Her friend replied, "I'm not afraid of dying," to which Deva replied, "No, you're afraid of living." Her friend was amazed and told Deva that she was right. I was amazed, too, and realized that Deva's own sense of right and wrong was more—much more—powerful than me telling her what to do or not do.

What's really difficult in these situations is keeping your heart open to the people who are not following their own sense of right and wrong without being pulled into the mistakes they are making. This, I believe, is one of the reasons it is so important to keep the lines of communication open with your children. The struggle they have as adolescents is moment to moment, and at any moment they could give into peer pressure, no matter how good your relationship is with them. There never seems to be a resting place. They will need you then more than ever. It's important to remember that your job now is not to make sure your children never make a mistake. I can guarantee they will; all of us do. Your job is to relate to them and understand what they need from you regardless of what they do. Some days that will be easier than others.

It's also important to remember that all of us develop at our own pace. You have to adjust your expectations to your child's needs and abilities. Some children take longer than others to learn new ways of behaving. Make sure you never compare your children to each other or another child. This will just get you and your children off track. Your job as a parent is to harmonize with your child—in other words, be compassionate, regardless of how long it takes your child to learn or if he never learns.

"How Do I Know If My Child Needs a Therapist?"

If you are wondering if your child needs a therapist in addition to the play sessions you are doing at home, it's probably best to play it safe and get a therapist's opinion. I can outline some of the signs and symptoms that would lead me to believe therapy might be helpful, but it's impossible to be completely thorough without meeting you and your child.

Some of the important questions you can ask yourself about your child that I might ask if you were in my office are:

1. Is your child eating and sleeping well?
2. Are bedtime, chore time, and homework time manageable?
3. Does your child have friends and get along well with other children?
4. Is your child doing well at school?
5. Is your child respectful to adults and peers?

If your child is having a problem in any of these areas that you feel you can't handle, then you should consult a therapist.

Obvious and more severe problems that would need immediate attention include:

1. Suicidal or homicidal thoughts, threats, or behavior
2. Self-mutilation, including cutting, scratching, pulling hair out, extreme dieting, extreme exercise, or binge eating
3. Drug or alcohol use
4. Being withdrawn, unwilling to communicate
5. Fear of something that is not usually considered scary

6. Sad, crying often, lethargic, low self-esteem

7. Anger outbursts, fighting, violent behavior or ideation

There are so many symptoms that could be severe that it would be impossible to list them all. If you are concerned about your child, though, and feel he needs help beyond what you can offer, it's important to get professional help as soon as possible.

I would also recommend consulting a therapist trained in filial therapy if your child seems stuck in play sessions. For example, if you child plays out the same scene in the dollhouse every session or only wants to play catch and nothing else, perhaps there is something you are missing. If your child repeatedly complains about play sessions, that might also be a sign that you need a consultation.

"How Do I Know If I Need Therapy?"

If you're wondering if you need therapy, then it might be a good idea to consult with a therapist. Generally speaking, if you're having trouble functioning in one of the major areas of your life, then it's probably time to seek help. The major areas include work, love, friends, family, eating, sleeping, and playing.

When you focus more intently on your child's needs, you are shifting your family system. The more dysfunctional the system, the more drastic the shift will be. One easy way to check if your family system is functioning well is to ask yourself, "Are we all behaving as though we're on the same side?" It may sound like a funny question to ask because obviously you're on the same side, but does your behavior communicate that? If you're keeping score, for example, saying, "Well, I wouldn't do that if you didn't do this" or "I only did that because you did this," you are not on the same side.

Other important questions to ask yourself to check the health of your family system are: Do I know what I need from my spouse? Do I know what my spouse needs from me? Do I know what my children need? If your child acts completely different during the play therapy session with you than outside of it, then it might be an indication of how things need to change in the family system. Perhaps some emotional need is being met in the session that isn't met outside the session. Sometimes practicing the play therapy model with your child can help you become aware of how difficult it is for you to focus on your child's needs. Without realizing it, we can look to our child to make us feel better, when what we need to do is grieve. The only reason we ever put our wishes before our children's emotional needs is because we don't know how to cope with the emotional pain we are feeling. In my opinion, that's the time to get some help.

A Word About Medication

It's fairly common knowledge that kids are overmedicated. Two of the most common misdiagnoses are ADHD and bipolar disorder, and the most common treatment for both of these diagnoses is medication. What I see in my practice is that the medication is usually not making that much difference after a few months. That's usually when parents come to see me, when the effects of the medication, or perhaps the novelty of the medication, wear off and the behaviors return. I'm biased of course, partly because of my experience. If the medication has done wonders and there are no more problems, I'm not going to see those kids. Why would I need to?

I have found many times that kids no longer need medication or need significantly less medication after their needs are better understood through the play therapy training their parents do. However, that is not always the case. Sometimes kids need help that only medication can provide. It's very difficult to know as a parent what is best for your child. My husband and I struggled a great deal in trying to understand what Dylan needed most, medication or to increase his ability to cope. Ultimately, we decided that building coping skills would serve him more than the medication. Sometimes both are needed, though.

Your Child's Diagnosis

I have seen some amazing transformations as a therapist just by training parents in this method. However, no treatment is the end-all and be-all. Regardless of your child's diagnosis, I believe that learning to relate in the ways described in this book can help meet your child's emotional needs. In my practice I have found these methods helpful for every child I've worked with. However, if your child has been diagnosed by a professional or is just noticeably different from other children in some way and should be diagnosed by a professional, other interventions may be necessary. For example, if your child is learning disabled, he will need a skilled teacher to help him learn. If your child has been abused or traumatized, it is very important to have her seen by a professional in addition to the play sessions you have with her. If your child is addicted to a substance or is part of a family system in which addiction is present, he may need a 12-step program. If your child is diagnosed with autism or Asperger's, she will need interventions to help shape her behavior so she can function better. There are probably other examples of essential interventions warranted by particular diagnoses. I'm sure I couldn't name them all.

Hopefully, as you have practiced this program, you have seen a shift in the way your child sees himself or herself. As you focus on the joy that your child brings you and the strengths your child has, your child will begin to understand how much he matters and how competent he is. As you learn to focus on being compassionate and meeting your child's needs, she will learn how to respect herself and take care of herself.

As I was finishing this book, Dylan called to read a poem he wrote. I think it describes the way our perception of ourselves, the world, and the people in it change each time we are able to accept a little more of ourselves and our experience, especially those parts of ourselves we have been afraid of. Our inner and outer worlds become one as we become willing to harmonize with whatever we come in contact with.

Dylan's Poem, November 9, 2007

I am so far inside myself, I cannot see out.

The world around me has become a momentary blur of clarity.

I feel as I did before the mountain,

the only difference is I'm completely present for it this time.

This is the feeling I was afraid of returning to and now I'm basking in it.

The world is like a glaze once more, but this time I can taste it.

I can hear it and smell it.

Sight is something of a game and sound is a startling maze of existence flashing in and out like a strobe light with no rhythm,

but with an eloquent precision and meaning.

Touch is a constant.

Notes

Introduction

1. Landreth, Garry, and Sue Bratton. *Child Parent Relationship Therapy (CPRT): A 10-Session Filial Therapy Model.* New York: Routledge, 2006.
2. Bratton, Sue, Garry Landreth, Theresa Kellam, and Sandra Blackard. *Child Parent Relationship Therapy (CPRT) Treatment Manual: A 10-Session Filial Therapy Model for Training Parents.* New York: Routledge, 2006.
3. I have obtained permission of the clients whose stories are used in this book or I have changed the story and details, combining information so that the clients are unrecognizable.

Chapter 1

1. Kellam, Theresa. "A Mother's Perspective on CPRT Training: Learning About My Child and Myself." In Garry Landreth and Sue Bratton, *Child Parent Relationship Therapy (CPRT): A 10-Session Filial Therapy Model.* New York: Routledge, 2006.
2. Bratton, Sue, Garry Landreth, Theresa Kellam, and Sandra Blackard. *Child Parent Relationship Therapy (CPRT) Treatment Manual: A 10-Session Filial Therapy Model for Training Parents.* New York: Routledge, 2006.
3. *Little Miss Sunshine.* Jonathon Dayton and Valerie Faris (directors). Greg Kinnear, Steve Carell, Toni Collette, Paul Dano, Abigail Breslin, and Alan Arkin (performers). DVD. 20th Century Fox, 2006.
4. Landreth, Garry, and Sue Bratton. *Child Parent Relationship Therapy (CPRT): A 10-Session Filial Therapy Model.* New York: Routledge, 2006.
5. Bratton, Sue, Garry Landreth, Theresa Kellam, and Sandra Blackard. *Child Parent Relationship Therapy (CPRT) Treatment Manual: A 10-Session Filial Therapy Model for Training Parents.* New York: Routledge, 2006.

Chapter 2

1. *Knocked Up.* Judd Apatow (director). Seth Rogen, Katherine Heigl, Paul Rudd, and Leslie Mann (performers). DVD. Universal, 2007.
2. Landreth, Garry. *Play Therapy: The Art of the Relationship.* 2nd ed. New York: Brunner-Routledge, 2002.
3. Landreth, Garry, and Sue Bratton. *Child Parent Relationship Therapy (CPRT): A 10-Session Filial Therapy Model.* New York: Routledge, 2006.
4. Allan, John. *Inscapes to the Child's World: Jungian Counseling in Schools and Clinics.* Dallas, TX: Spring Publications, 1988.
5. Kellam, Theresa. "A Mother's Perspective on CPRT Training: Learning About My Child and Myself." In Garry Landreth and Sue Bratton, *Child Parent Relationship Therapy (CPRT): A 10-Session Filial Therapy Model.* New York: Routledge, 2006.
6. Bratton, Sue, Garry Landreth, Theresa Kellam, and Sandra Blackard. *Child Parent Relationship Therapy (CPRT) Treatment Manual: A 10-Session Filial Therapy Model for Training Parents.* New York: Routledge, 2006.

Chapter 3

1. The ideas in this chapter come from Garry Landreth and Sue Bratton. *Child Parent Relationship Therapy (CPRT): A 10-Session Filial Therapy Model.* New York: Routledge, 2006; and Bratton, Sue, Garry Landreth, Theresa Kellam, and Sandra Blackard. *Child Parent Relationship Therapy (CPRT) Treatment Manual: A 10-Session Filial Therapy Model for Training Parents.* New York: Routledge, 2006.
2. Bratton, Sue, Garry Landreth, Theresa Kellam, and Sandra Blackard. *Child Parent Relationship Therapy (CPRT) Treatment Manual: A 10-Session Filial Therapy Model for Training Parents.* New York: Routledge, 2006.
2a. Guerney, L. (1972). *Filial Therapy: A Training Manual for Parents.* Unpublished manuscript. (Don'ts 1–7 are taken from Guerney, 1972.)
3. Landreth, Garry, and Sue Bratton. *Child Parent Relationship Therapy (CPRT): A 10-Session Filial Therapy Model.* New York: Routledge, 2006.
4. Blackard, Sandra. *Say What You See for Parents and Teachers.* 2nd ed. [Brochure] Round Rock, TX: Author, 2007.

5. Developed by the Center for Play Therapy at the University of North Texas in Denton, Texas.

6. Kellam, Theresa. "A Mother's Perspective on CPRT Training: Learning About My Child and Myself." In Garry Landreth and Sue Bratton, *Child Parent Relationship Therapy (CPRT): A 10-Session Filial Therapy Model.* New York: Routledge, 2006.

Chapter 4

1. Cited by Karen, Robert, *Becoming Attached: First Relationships and How They Shape Our Capacity to Love.* New York: Oxford, 1994, p. 5.

2. Chödrön, Pema. *The Places That Scare You: A Guide to Fearlessness in Difficult Times.* Boston, MA: Shambhala, 2001.

3. Linehan, Marsha. *Cognitive-Behavioral Treatment for Borderline Personality Disorder and Skills Training Manual for Treating Borderline Personality Disorder.* New York: Guilford Press, 1993.

4. Bratton, Sue, Garry Landreth, Theresa Kellam, and Sandra Blackard. *Child Parent Relationship Therapy (CPRT) Treatment Manual: A 10-Session Filial Therapy Model for Training Parents.* New York: Routledge, 2006.

Chapter 5

1. Bratton, Sue, Garry Landreth, Theresa Kellam, and Sandra Blackard. *Child Parent Relationship Therapy (CPRT) Treatment Manual: A 10-Session Filial Therapy Model for Training Parents.* New York: Routledge, 2006.

Chapter 6

1. *Choices, Cookies and Kids.* Center for Play Therapy (producer). Garry Landreth (performer). DVD. The Center for Play Therapy, 2004.

2. Bratton, Sue, Garry Landreth, Theresa Kellam, and Sandra Blackard. *Child Parent Relationship Therapy (CPRT) Treatment Manual: A 10-Session Filial Therapy Model for Training Parents.* New York: Routledge, 2006.

3. Roberts, Monty. *Horse Sense for People*. New York: Penguin, 2002.

Chapter 7

1. Kellam, Theresa. "A Mother's Perspective On CPRT Training: Learning About My Child and Myself." In Garry Landreth and Sue Bratton, *Child Parent Relationship Therapy (CPRT): A 10-Session Filial Therapy Model*. New York: Routledge, 2006.
2. *Family Guy Presents Stewie Griffin: The Untold Story*. Peter Michels and Peter Shin (directors). Seth MacFarlane, Alex Borstein, Seth Green, and Mila Kunis (performers). DVD. 20th Century Fox, 2005.
3. Bratton, Sue, Garry Landreth, Theresa Kellam, and Sandra Blackard. *Child Parent Relationship Therapy (CPRT) Treatment Manual: A 10-Session Filial Therapy Model for Training Parents*. New York: Routledge, 2006.

Chapter 8

1. Blackard, Sandra. *Say What You See for Parents and Teachers*. 2nd ed. [Brochure]. Round Rock, TX: Author, 2007.
2. Nichols, Michael, and Richard Schwartz. *Family Therapy: Concepts and Methods*. 4th ed. Boston, MA: Allyn and Bacon, 1998.
3. Landreth, Garry. "Therapeutic Limit Setting in the Play Therapy Relationship." *Professional Psychology: Research and Practice*, 33 (2002): 529–535.
4. Bratton, Sue, Garry Landreth, Theresa Kellam, and Sandra Blackard. *Child Parent Relationship Therapy (CPRT) Treatment Manual: A 10-Session Filial Therapy Model for Training Parents*. New York: Routledge, 2006.

Chapter 9

1. Chödrön, Pema. *The Places That Scare You: A Guide to Fearlessness in Difficult Times*. Boston, MA: Shambhala, 2001.
2. Bratton, Sue, Garry Landreth, Theresa Kellam, and Sandra Blackard. *Child Parent Relationship Therapy (CPRT) Treatment Manual: A 10-Session Filial Therapy Model for Training Parents*. New York: Routledge, 2006.

3. Mortola, Peter. *Window Frames: Learning Gestalt Therapy the Oaklander Way.* New York: Routledge, 2006.

Chapter 10

1. Allan, John. *Inscapes to the Child's World: Jungian Counseling in Schools and Clinics.* Dallas, TX: Spring Publications, 1988.
2. Kellam, Theresa. "A Mother's Perspective on CPRT Training: Learning About My Child and Myself." In Garry Landreth and Sue Bratton, *Child Parent Relationship Therapy (CPRT): A 10-Session Filial Therapy Model.* New York: Routledge, 2006.